THE ENGLAND OF SHAKESPEARE.

AMS PRESS
NEW YORK

THE HOUSE AT STRATFORD-ON-AVON WHERE SHAKESPEARE WAS BORN.

THE

ENGLAND OF SHAKESPEARE.

BY

EDWIN GOADBY.

New Edition, with Illustrations.

CASSELL & COMPANY, LIMITED:

LONDON, PARIS, NEW YORK & MELBOURNE.

ion Data

Reprint of the 1881 ed.
1. Shakespeare, William, 1564-1616—Contemporary England. 2. England—Social life and customs—16th century. I. Title
PR2910.G57 1973 822.3'3 76-168169
ISBN 0-404-02839-X

Reprinted from the 1881 edition, London and New York
First AMS edition published in 1973
Manufactured in the United States of America

AMS PRESS INC.
NEW YORK, N.Y. 10003

PREFACE.

THE title of this volume may perhaps seem more ambitious than its contents. A new history of the period may be expected, with elaborate criticisms on its statesmen and its policy, or a new life of Shakespeare, with especial reference to his ancestors or his sonnets. The selection of the title, however, has been made with a strict regard to the aim and the nature of the work. It is not a history so much as a description. If there be anything like a theory in its pages, nothing more startling will be found than the notion that every great mind is more or less rooted in its own age, no matter how high it may tower, or with what leafy richness it may spread and poise its branches. General histories cannot deal very extensively with social features, and special histories are apt to sacrifice breadth and pictorial effect to elaborate narrative and exhaustive analysis. In the face of both, there still appears to be room for a concise and fairly complete account of the England in which our great poet lived, wrote, and died. No adequate biography of Shakespeare is possible, and hence the general craving for a study of his surroundings, which shall be faithful without being tedious, and historical without being ordinary history. Accordingly, we present here a companion volume to more elaborate works as well as a guide to the study of Shakespeare himself, and a substitute, wherever it may be desired, for the prickly controversies which must always mark textual criticism and transcendental research. Possibly, to some persons the result may seem "base, common, and popular." But care has been taken to supplement the results of acknowledged authorities with the fruits of independent study; and the absence of foot-notes and references ought not to alarm the critic, and will certainly not displease the reader. In handling such a mass of minute details it is hardly possible that the method adopted will always satisfy the possessors of what Bacon calls "over-delicate learning;" at the same time the author hopes they will recognise the general aim of the work, and the spirit in which he has endeavoured to execute it.

CONTENTS.

CHAPTER I.

INTRODUCTORY.

PAGE

General Conditions of England in Shakespeare's Time — The Something Statistics could not Show—Foreign Opinion of Englishmen—Unique Character of Shakespeare—Description of his Age Necessary—Brief Summary 13

CHAPTER II.

APPEARANCE OF THE COUNTRY.

Ports, Cities, and Towns—Country Villages, Churches, Roads, Bridges, and Inns—Postal Communication—The Decaying Woods — Enclosures — Local Products — The Fens — The Castles and Mansions 19

CHAPTER III.

TRADE AND COMMERCE.

English Wool and Corn — Coins — Merchant Adventurers and Foreign Trading Companies—English Woollens and Cloths —The New Trades Introduced by French and Flemish Immigrants — Coal and Metal Industries — Monopolies — The Pawn-banks 38

PAGE

CHAPTER IV.

MARITIME DEVELOPMENT.

Royal Influence—The Fisheries—Privateering and Smuggling—The Viking Temper—Frobisher—Davis—Cavendish—The Hawkinses — Sir John Gilbert—Sir Francis Drake — Sir Walter Raleigh—Sir Richard Grenville - English Vitality . 51

CHAPTER V.

GENERAL CHARACTERISTICS—ARMY AND NAVY.

Extravagance in Costume—Ladies' and Gentlemen's Attire—Cutting the Hair—Dress and Class—Manners—Duels and Street Rows—Life in Country Mansions—Food and Cooks—Few Vegetables in Use—Consumption of Beer and Wine—Taking Tobacco — Domestic Interiors — Amusements and Sports—Archery—The Surveys and Musters—Imperfect Military Training—The Armada Enrolments—The Two Fleets—English Eagerness—Drake's Summary of the Fight with Spain 71

CHAPTER VI.

RELIGION AND EDUCATION.

Legal Establishment of Protestantism—New Hopes—The Condition of Churches and Parishes—Gradual and Imperfect Changes—The Catholic Party—Preaching and Prophesying—Psalms and Surplices—Introduction of Pews—Puritanism—The New Poor Law—Universities and Grammar Schools—Education and Travel—Ignorance of the Common People 102

CHAPTER VII.

SCIENCE AND SUPERSTITION.

Unscientific Character of the Elizabethans—Bruno, Bacon, and the Copernican System — Gilbert, Harvey, and Medical

PAGE

Science—Whims of the Learned—Popular Medicine—Royal Cures—Precious Stones as Charms—Astrology—Dr. Dee—Alchemy—The Belief in Witchcraft—Laws Against it—Shakespearean Witches—Spirits—Wonders and Omens—Telling Ghost-stories—Plants, Animals, and Days—Impossible for Shakespeare to Escape such Influences 117

CHAPTER VIII.

THE COURT—ELIZABETH AND JAMES I.

The Courts of Elizabeth and James True Mirrors of the Time—The Difference of *Personnel*—The Royal Palaces—The Royal Progresses—Elizabeth's Ceremonialism—Love of Dress and Ornament—Personal Appearance—Learning—Compliments—Money Matters—James I. 134

CHAPTER IX.

SHAKESPEARE'S LONDON.

The City a Wonder—Its External Appearance—The River and its Mansions—Alsatia—Bankside and its Associations—London Bridge—A Stroll with Jonson and Shakespeare—Fish Hill—East Chepe—London Stone—The Exchange—Cheapside—The "Mermaid Tavern"—St. Paul's—Fleet Street—General Impressions 151

CHAPTER X.

THE DRAMA.

Miracle and Guild Plays—Interludes and Masks—Royal Players—Companies of Children—The Pageants—Court Revels—Strolling Players—Inn-yard Theatres—Noblemen's Companies—The First London Theatres—A Peep at the Globe during Play-time—Poverty of Dress and Scenery—Parts Played by Shakespeare—Purpose of the Stage 173

PAGE

CHAPTER XI.

LITERATURE OF THE PERIOD.

Its Excellence—A Revelation to Europe—Euphuism the Counterpart of Fantastic Dress—Shakespeare's Miscellaneous Reading—His Indebtedness to Others—The Solid Works of the Time—Pamphlets—Miscellaneous Poetry—Spenser—Dramatic Literature Nearest Popular Heart—Early Dramas—Shakespeare's Contemporaries—His Sudden Rise to Eminence—Contemporary Allusions—Complete View not possible in his Lifetime—The England of his Birth and Death . . . 201

THE

ENGLAND OF SHAKESPEARE

CHAPTER I.

INTRODUCTORY.

General Conditions of England in Shakespeare's Time—The Something Statistics could not Show—Foreign Opinion of Englishmen—Unique Character of Shakespeare—Description of his Age Necessary—Brief Summary.

THE England of Shakespeare would have sorely puzzled the modern statistician. Had he lived in the period before the Armada, he would have found no warrant in his figures for that signal triumph, and had he belonged to the period after it he would have pondered as long and as dolefully as the owl in Mr. Froude's fable, which consumed its nights in musing as to which came first, the egg or the bird. The facts of the Elizabethan age which can be expressed in tables of figures are very mean and paltry. Omitting Ireland and Scotland, the population of the country was not greater than the present population of London. The land was fertile, but it was imperfectly cultivated. There were no very large towns to act as reservoirs of national feeling, to warn an erring monarch, and to sustain a vacillating government. London and Bristol, Norwich and York,

Plymouth and Coventry, were separated by long reaches of wild land and bad roads. They were practically as far apart as Paris and Madrid, Berlin and Vienna, Rome and Athens, are at the present day. The construction of one of our monster iron-clads would have absorbed the annual national revenue of those times.

The nobles were still rich and powerful, the middle classes were rising into prominence, the common people were scattered and poor. The army, when called into existence, was a medley of military survivals. Billmen and archers, pikemen and harquebusiers, some in armour and others in stuff tunics, shouldered each other in the national array. The navy was scanty and ill-manned, the vessels hardly equal to our medium-sized coasters, the sailors armed, for the most part, with bows and arrows, the cannon of primitive construction and of short range. The fame of the country had suffered in the contraction of its Continental power. Its enemies were numerous. The Pope was threatening, France doubtful, Spain hostile, Ireland always in rebellion, the Scotch troublesome and intriguing. The country was divided by religious faction, noble exiles were openly supported by foreign Courts, and trade languished. The destinies of the nation were in the hands of a woman who had many whims, many wooers, and more personal favourites than were good for her peace of mind or the contentment of her people.

The something statistics could not completely show, even if they tabulated the men of mark in politics, literature, and science, was the character of the people. "Walled towns, stored arsenals and armouries, goodly races of horses, elephants, ordnance, artillery, and the like—all this," said Lord Bacon, "is but a sheep in a lion's skin except the breed and disposition of the people be stout and warlike." The Elizabethan Englishmen were noted for their personal stoutness and hardihood. Their pluck was undoubted. "As fierce as an Englishman" was a French proverb long before George Whetstone embodied the saying in a poetical preface to his martial volume. The Dutch thought them lazy and given to spectacle; they were "fond of great ear-filling noises, such as cannon-firing, drum-beating, and bell-ringing," says Meteren. "Handsome and well-shaped," according to Paul Hentzner, the German, they were also "stout-hearted, vehement, eager, cruel in war, zealous in attack, little fearing death; not revengeful, but fickle, presumptuous, rash, boastful, deceitful; very suspicious, especially of strangers." Evidently a people capable of great things, but not yet appraised at their true value, or shaped with the lineaments of a settled and solid character. They had yet to show "the mettle of their pasture," in battle and adventure, on sea and land, in literature and the arts.

But how the time and the land ever came to produce William Shakespeare will always be somewhat of a marvel. Shakespeare's father was a yeoman, and anything but a man of marked culture. Splendid opportunities, rare teachers, enthusiastic companions, will sometimes kindle the flame that flashes into genius.

Until he had become known as a poet, and his character was set, Shakespeare had none of these. A great man will sometimes be the receptive pupil of another, who may be too infirm, too roughly-nurtured, to convey his message to the world. Shakespeare had no such advantage. He lived amongst men whose fame was already half established, and yet thrust himself easily over their heads and shoulders. Other men have left behind them diaries, letters, memoirs, wasting a world of industry over morbid self-dissection and intellectual flickerings. Shakespeare lives in his works. His age is there; his secret is there.

Sometimes the man makes the age, and at others the age creates the man. No one has yet contended that Shakespeare made his age, but perhaps we do not understand as clearly as we might the part played by the age in limning and moulding him. He was not its creature, and yet the features of the age have left their impress on everything he wrote. His dramas and comedies seem to have been written in the street and the public tavern rather than in the closet, so rich are they in contemporary references, in slang expressions, sly hits, snatches of ballads, descriptions of living characters, and all the wit and humour of the time. A description of his age is therefore an essential part of any estimate of the man. It may relieve us of elaborate theorising; it may be the best explanation attainable by the average understanding. To know the surroundings of a man is to come so much nearer to the man himself, to see things with his eyes, and almost to touch that untold life which throbs within and behind his works, like the inner brightness that seems ever glowing from beneath the surface of the purest marble.

It is not enough to chat about his birth and marriage, the dates of his works and the number of his rhymed lines. Nor is it very helpful to narrate the full story of the age, as it is found in histories and Court biographies. We may understand all that touched Queen Elizabeth or King James, and yet be as far off as ever from living in their England, from striking hands with Shakespeare, and looking into his serene brown eyes. What we know of his external life is very limited. Born at Stratford-on-Avon, educated at the grammar-school there, possibly an usher in the school, he married there, went to London about 1587, played the several parts of actor, author, and manager, bought property in his native town, retired there, and died at the age of fifty-two, leaving behind him a wife and two children. The portraits of him all give us the impression of a handsome man, robust and well-shaped, kindly-natured, gentle in spirit, subtle in intelligence. His face is not that of a closet-student, weighted with the authority of his own masters, and haunted by perplexing moral casuistries. It is that of a man of the world, living largely and generously amongst his fellows, reading their characters and touched by their foibles, and of opulent understanding as to everything reported or visible to the mighty world of ear and eye.

Between 1564 and 1614 English history was a mixed panorama. Mary Queen of Scots had fled to

England, had plotted, and had been beheaded. Elizabeth had been sought in marriage by Ivan the Terrible, Philip of Spain, and the Duke of Alençon. Her subjects had wished her to marry, and one Court favourite after another had seemed eager to claim her hand. The religious struggles of the time had ripened into Uniformity at home and into wars and intrigues abroad. The Netherlands had revolted, Ireland had risen in bloody rebellion, and Spain had made a mighty portentous effort to conquer England. The attempt had failed, England had come off conqueror, and a new era had opened with "*réveilles* to the breaking morn." After Elizabeth and her statesmen had come James and his feeble time-servers. Witty and weak, he had wished to play the despot, and he had not always been able to restrain either himself or his subjects.

In the several chapters of this work we shall set forth only so much of general history as will serve to illustrate the central figure, of whom we shall say little, but suggest much. What we seek to obtain is a vivid glance into the life and rhythmic movements of the time.

CHAPTER II.

APPEARANCE OF THE COUNTRY.

Ports, Cities, and Towns—Country Villages, Churches, Roads, Bridges, and Inns—Postal Communication—The Decaying Woods—Enclosures—Local Products—The Fens—The Castles and Mansions.

THE "nook-shotten isle of England," at the time of which we are writing, was indented with bays and harbours, but most of them were without piers and landing-places. The arrangements for navigation were most primitive, buoys and lighthouses being unknown, and beacon-fires, pitch-pots, and lights on church towers, serving to direct the mariner at night. Plymouth, Bristol, Chester, Southampton, Portsmouth, Dover, London, Yarmouth, Hull, and Newcastle, were the principal ports; London will have to be described by itself presently. The interior of the country did not greatly impress the traveller. Twenty-six cities were said to be in existence, all girdled by walls and towers, famous for churches, rich with antiquities, busy with the hum of commercial life. Older places, like York and Bristol, had once had quite a suburb of monasteries and abbeys, with their pretty grounds and salad-growing gardens. The buildings remained, and so did the garden-grounds; but the former were untenanted, the latter untrimmed. Chester, Taunton, Norwich, Coventry, and other places, were full of empty decaying houses, owing to the ravages of epidemics, the fluctuations of trade, and the greater security of life and property attainable in the open country.

Wooden houses were common, with overhanging upper storeys; the older ones with windows of horn and lattice-work, the newer with glass. Brick and stone were coming into more general use, however, and foreign workmen were employed in building because they worked for lower wages. "If ever curious building did flourish in England," says Harrison, "it is in these our years, wherein our workmen excel, and are in manner comparable in skill with old Vitruvius, Leo Baptiste, and Serlo." But he was thinking more of the fine mansions of the nobility—of which more anon—than of the houses in the provincial towns, most of which were thatched with reeds. In 1583 the Corporation of Norwich ordered reeds to be discontinued for tiles, slates, and lead. Cornwall furnished thin slabs for roofing, while in clayey districts tiles prevailed, and in Leicestershire, slates. The houses of franklins and local gentry were enclosed with walls and ornamented with balconies, parapets, turrets, and gable ends. The house-fronts were carved with humorous devices, or paned with oaken woodwork, or whitened with mortar and plaster. The streets were narrow, irregular, and without causeways; full of refuse, and lively with pigs, poultry, and ravenous birds. Some corporate towns endeavoured to be more strict, and forbade live stock without attendants. The water supply was from wells, or ran in open conduits or wooden pipes, to the market cross or public fountain. Leaden pipes were only invented in 1538, and were a long time coming into general use.

Outside the towns the country was for the most part open and unenclosed, dotted with what Shakespeare speaks of as "poor pelting (paltry) villages, sheepcotes, and mills"; the villages built in straggling fashion round a large green, with its may-pole and its open pool. Outside the villages, in snug demesnes, were the manor-houses of the country squires: timbered residences with plenty of fruit-trees behind them, and much comfort within. The solemn yew-trees standing by threw a shade pleasant in the summer-time. Norman, Perpendicular, and even less pretentious village churches, with their trim-kept graveyards, and ancient monuments within of cross-legged Crusaders and local families, gave a pleasant aspect to a richly-wooded landscape. The heavy handle on the church door, still to be met with in many cases, was for the benefit of fugitive criminals, who clung to it until the door was opened, and they could obtain sanctuary for forty days, with leave to embark for some foreign country in case their crime had been murder. In 1575 there were 8,911 parish churches in the realm, besides chapels and churches in the dioceses of Bristol and Oxford not included in the return.

There were, or professed to be, high roads between the principal towns, maintained at the expense of the Crown. They were rarely repaired, and Shakespeare's audiences must have relished the wit of Gratiano, in *The Merchant of Venice*, when he exclaimed—

> "Why this is like the mending of highways
> In summer, where the roads are fair enough."

Ruts, bogs, and holes, were referred to in all the common saws. The epithet "deep" applied to them by Shrewsbury is very expressive. When Mary Queen of Scots was removed from Bolton Castle to Ripon, on her way south, the journey of sixteen miles took her from early morning to late in the evening of a January day, owing to the "foule, long and cumbersome" road. Travelling was consequently limited to the wealthy, and was even a feat. A rhyming pamphleteer of the day says :—

> "A citizen, for recreation sake,
> To see the country would a journey take
> Some dozen miles, or very little more,
> Taking his leave with friends two months before,
> With drinking healths, and shaking by the hand,
> As he had travelled to some new-found land."

On the main roads there were substantial bridges, some built by pious priests of an earlier time ; others with legends about them, like the one over the Lune, in Westmoreland, said to have been built by the devil ; and a few of a more recent date, due to private munificence or local enterprise. If of stone, they were usually narrow and steep, except in places where they covered shallow and easily-flooded rivers, when they were many-arched, flat, and had houses and chantries upon them. In some cases the bridge-masters were the most important local officials, and fairs were held upon the bridges, as was the first cloth-fair which gave its celebrity to Brig-gate in Leeds. Many bridges were merely of stone pillars, with oaken beams placed across them, and had no parapets. No wholly wooden bridges were erected after 1591. The famous Rialto of Venice was built of alder hardened in water, but oak was generally used in England. Small foot-bridges were made of a single balk of timber with nailed cross-pieces, such as may still be seen in the Yorkshire dales, where Chaucer's speech still lingers. The foul fiend who tormented poor Tom, in *King Lear*, made him "proud of heart to ride on a bay trotting-horse over four-inch bridges."

Winding over marshy moors, amidst boulders and through dense woods, the unfenced roads were marked by derelict vehicles to remind the traveller of his peril, as the bones of pilgrims on an Eastern track quicken his sense of piety. The roads made themselves, but the general idea was to have them hollow in the centre. An ingenious writer issued a pamphlet proposing to mend highways by laying down frames of wood and hurdles, filling up the spaces, and covering them over with broken stones and rubbish. This pamphlet was addressed to King James, with a poetical preface, and illustrated by many diagrams.

Splendid hostelries existed on the great thoroughfares, able to accommodate three hundred guests, their horses and servants. Harrison says, with these houses in his mind, that of "all inns in England there were no worse than in London." In these excellently-furnished inns, with their gorgeous signboards, the traveller touched all kinds of life. Here he would meet the nobleman, with a small army of servants, carrying half of his furniture with him as he moved from place to place; the knight of the shire or the burgess on his way to London, spending his allowance of 2s. a day and expenses for what was quaintly called "knight's meat," and "citizen's meat"; the poor scholar on his way to Oxford or the Temple, his cob and himself a compound of leanness and learning; or perhaps a bishop, attended by his chaplains, with hawks and hounds for his diversion by the way; the fashionable highwayman; the suitor bound for Westminster or York; wounded soldiers, romancing sailors, musical tinkers, and weary foot-passengers, paying a penny a night for their beds. Many scenes of this kind must Shakespeare have witnessed at Stratford, as the traffic stayed there between Oxford and Birmingham.

There was little postal communication, except for the service of the Crown, in the early part of the period. Queen Mary had arranged a regular service between London and Berwick, and a letter so sent was three or four days on the road. A second service had grown up between London and Dover. Usually, letter-writers sent their own messengers, or trusted to the lumbering stage-waggons, which were something like furniture vans, with only a door for light and ventilation, and went westward as far as Exeter and northward as far as York, at about two miles an hour. In 1568, however, the Queen discharged all posts, "except the posts of the Court," that would not serve for half their former wages. Enterprising Corporations were put upon their mettle, and arranged posts of their own. Norwich set up post-horses, and lent money to start the postmasters. A horse was not to carry more than a 10lb. bag, to travel for less than 6d. a mile outwards, or to go more than fourteen miles in a journey. The necessary guide was to receive 6d. a mile. To London "every one was to agree as he could." After the Armada, a horse-post was ordered to be established in every town, and a foot-post in every parish, who was to live "near the church." But nothing effective was done until King James took the matter in hand. A letter from Lynn to London, about ninety miles in a bee-line, cost 26s. 8d. The bustle on the North road, immediately after his arrival in London, is said to have called the King's attention to the posts. Scotchmen, anxious for preferment, swarmed from Edinburgh to London, paralysing the ordinary traffic. He created a Postmaster-General for foreign parts, materially improving general communication. The running-posts were not established until after Shakespeare's death. It was in 1635 that fixed charges were made of 2d. a single sheet for under 80 miles, 4d. for 140 miles, 6d. for longer distances, and 8d. to Scotland.

Only one-fourth of the land was under cultivation. The remainder consisted of forests, mosses, and commons. Shakespeare makes Ceres refer, in *The Tempest*, to "bosky acres and unshrubbed downs." In Elizabeth's time there were eighty-six forests in England, although some were becoming mere names; our moors are the only vestiges left by many of them

Only fifteen of the forty English counties were destitute of woods, and they were chiefly on the east and south-east coast. Some of the forests were of great extent. Arden had formerly reached from the Severn to the Trent; Sherwood extended into Yorkshire; Dean was dense and large until iron-mining commenced. But Dartmoor was getting bare, and Drayton described the Peak Forest as "the model of the Arabian stony wild." "Goodly Gautries," as he calls it, extended from the Hambleton Hills right up to York, and Shakespeare places in it several scenes in the Second Part of *Henry IV.* James I. built himself a hunting lodge in its recesses. The picture in the "Fairy Queen" fairly represents the older forests:—

> "Not perceable with power of any starr,
> And all within were pathes and alleies wide,
> With footing worne, and leading inward farre."

The whole poem is a woodland romance. The southern woods had suffered more than those in the north, owing to greater density of population. Hayward states that when St. Paul's Cathedral was burnt down, in 1561, "the new and strong timber for its roof was framed in Yorkshire, and by sea conveyed to London; the charges of which work amounted to the sum of £5,982 13s. 4d."

Beech had formerly been abundant in Berkshire, Oxfordshire, and Buckinghamshire. It was in great demand. Coachmakers bought it at 7d. per foot. The smaller trees were cut up into faggots for bakers and household use. Large quantities were sent to London for the ships. Each billet was notched, and the woodsman received 6d. for every 255 notches, or a load. Sizes were regulated by statute. An old rhymer wrote :—

> "Beech made their chests, their beds, and the joined stools ;
> Beech made the board, the platters, and the bowls."

Walnut grew in the south, and was freely used for bedsteads until displaced by foreign mahogany. Oak wainscot was displaced in a similar way, not because it was getting scarce, as some writers have inferred, but because finer-grained and whiter timber was coming in from Spain and Norway, better suited for panels. Yew-trees grew about the houses, and were chiefly used for bows.

The oak-tree was rapidly disappearing from the virgin woods. On the Continent this fact has been traced to the planting of the beech, which overtops and finally supersedes both the oak and the birch. The value of our oak-forests was recognised by our enemies, who attributed to them our maritime greatness. "I have heard," remarks Evelyn, "that in the great expedition of 1588 it was expressly enjoined the Spanish commanders of that signal Armada, that if, when landed, they should not be able to subdue our nation, and make good their conquest, they should yet be sure not to leave a tree standing in the Forest of Dean." Splendid trees in this still extensive forest were regularly marked for the navy. Popular legends and regrets clustered about the oak. Lovers met under its boughs, fairies gambolled there, and the tree was associated with the sports of the chase, the nature of the people. Famous oaks were still in existence in Shakespeare's time. Drayton is full of piteous laments over the decaying woods. They were associated in his mind with the poetic past, with the beautiful fairies :—

> "Exiled their sweet abode, to poor bare commons fled,
> They with the oaks that lived now with the oaks are dead."

Another poet attributed their destruction to one cause alone :—

> "Woods, tall and reverend, from all time appear
> Inviolable, where no mine is near."

This was hardly the fact, for woods were consumed for fuel quite irrespectively of mines. They were also felled by their owners to provide the means for their luxurious living. But no doubt the mines aided in the destruction. "The exorbitance and devouring increase of iron-mills, unless looked into," remonstrated Evelyn, "will ruin old England." As a sample of old-time prophecy this is as good as any we could select. Elizabeth encouraged planting, and forbade grazing in the woods, but to little purpose. Even the use of coal did not check destruction. Shakespeare's *As You Like It* was charmingly devised to suit the temper of the poetic souls who invested the woods with foreshadowings of Rousseau's naturalism, whilst pleasantly contrasting court-life and shepherd-life for the benefit of others who, if they had not Jacques' melancholy, had some of Touchstone's wit. To "fleet the time carelessly as they did in the golden world" might require the primeval forests that were departing. But "'tis Hymen peoples every town," and the "shrewd days and nights" spent with oaks, harts, and hinds, simply served to lead to a truer happiness and a larger state.

There were not so many divisions on the surface of the landscape as now. Ploughed fields were divided by a ridge or baulk of earth. Old writers on husbandry call these open fields the "campion country," corrupting the well-known French term. Quickset hedges represent the turning of arable into pasture. The enclosure movement had begun in earlier reigns, but its force was unspent. Elizabeth passed several statutes to prevent it, but in vain. Hundreds of acres were left to a shepherd, his sheep, and dog. At Norwich, in 1611, a mutiny was threatened, "on the pretence, as in other places, of hindering new enclosures." Even at Stratford, under the eye of Shakespeare, who was a Welcombe freeholder, it was proposed to enclose that common. The corporation opposed, and in a page of his cousin Thomas Greene's diary, September 1, 1615, it is written, "Mr. Shakespeare told Mr. J. Greene that he was not able to bear the enclosuring of Welcombe." The movement was defeated.

In Devonshire fences were just coming into use; apple-trees were also being planted for cider in hedgerows and orchards. Gerard, an old writer, was most enthusiastic over this new venture. It was said the common people would break the fences and rob the fruit. "But forward," he says; "in the name of God, graff, set, plant, and nourish up trees in every corner of your ground; the labour is small, the cost is nothing, the commodity great; yourselves shall have the plenty, the poor shall have somewhat in time of want to relieve their necessity, and God shall reward your good minds and diligence." The pear-tree was grown in Gloucester, and also the grape-vine. Drayton refers to the "chalky Chiltern Hills"; to Taunton's "fruitful dean"; to the "fertile fields of Hereford"; to Northampton's "fattening pastures"; to Nottingham's "flowery meads"; to the fens, fair women, hounds, and large-horned hairy cattle of Lancashire; to the "mighty ships" of Newcastle; to Yorkshire as "an epitome" of everything in the island; to the "rich meads" of Cambridge; and to "hemp-bearing Holland's fen" (Lincolnshire). Harrison says the Dee was famous for its trout; the Yorkshire Ouse for a "verie sweet, fat and delicate" salmon; and the Thames for its fish of all kinds. The Trent was the paradise of anglers.

In his rhymed description of England, Drayton endeavours to illustrate what were then known to be the peculiarities of the English counties. Helidon bids them say what they can do, and their answers are worth giving as showing no change, in some cases, between past and present conditions, and most important alterations in others:—

"Kent first in our account doth to itself apply,
Quoth he this blazon first, 'Long tails and liberty!'
Sussex with Surrey say, 'Then let us lead home logs,'
As Hampshire long for her hath had the term of hogs.
So Dorsetshire of long they 'Dossers' used to call,
Cornwall and Devon say, 'We'll wrestle for a fall.'
Then Somerset says, 'Set the barn-dog on the bull,'

And Gloucestershire again is blazoned, 'Weigh thy wool';
As Berkshire hath for hers, 'Let's to't and toss the ball,'
And Wiltshire will for her, 'Get home and pay for all.'
Rich Buckingham doth bear the term of 'Bread and Beef,'
Where if you beat a bush 'tis odds you start a thief.
So Hertford blazoned is 'The club and clouted shoon,'
Thereto, 'I'll rise betimes and sleep again at noon';
When Middlesex bids, 'Up to London let us go,
And when our market's done, we'll have a pot or two';
As Essex hath of old been named, 'Calves and stiles,'
Fair Suffolk 'maids and mild,' and Norfolk 'many wiles,'
So Cambridge hath been called, 'Hold nets and let us win,'
And Huntingdon, 'With stilts we'll stalk through thick and thin.'
Northamptonshire of long hath had this blazon—'Love
Below the girdle all, but little else above!'
An outcry Oxford makes, 'The scholars have been here,
And little though they've pay'd, yet they have had good cheer';
Quoth warlike Warwick's line, 'I'll bind the sturdy bear,'
Quoth Wor'stershire again, 'And I will squirt the pear';
Then Staffordshire bids 'Stay, and I will beat the fire,
And nothing will I ask but goodwill for my hire.'
'Bean-belly' Leicestershire her attribute doth bear,
And 'Bells and bagpipes' next belong to Lincolnshire.
Of 'Malt-horse' Bedfordshire long since the blazon ran,
And little Rutlandshire is termed 'Raddleman';
To Derby is assigned the name of 'Wool and lead,'
As Nottingham of old (is common) 'Ale and bread';
So Hereford for her says, 'Give me woof and warp,'
And Shropshire saith in her, 'That shins be ever sharp,
Lay wood upon the fire, reach hither me my harp,
And while the black bowl walks we merrily will carp';
Of Cheshire is well known to be the 'chief of men,'
Fair women doth belong to Lancashire again;
The lands that Ouse to Berwick forth do bear,
Have for their blazon had, 'Snaffle, spur, and spear.'"

The fens of Lincolnshire have become almost legendary. They were once extensive and troublesome; the sea was always encroaching. Farmers were cut off for days together, and had to use boats and stilts. Flocks of ducks, mallard, teal, gossanders, widgeon, water-hens, dab-chicks, cranes, and bitterns, were common. In 1576 the Council wrote to the Commissioners of Sewers, then a new authority, instructing them to aid in levying a rate in their respective adjacent counties, to assist the inhabitants of the Isle of Ely in embanking, cleansing, and scouring "the river of Wisbeach." The Yarmouth people lost their navigation owing to the sand, and called in the assistance of Joyse Johnson, a Dutch engineer, who piled the Yare for them. In 1606 a Frenchman undertook to drain 300,000 acres on receiving 12,000 acres when his work was finished. Hatfield Chase was drained by Cornelius Vermuyden, and hundreds of Flemings settled in the land they had reclaimed in the Isle of Axholme Smeaton and Rennie, in a subsequent century, completed these works. As more land was drained, the use of rushes for house-floors was discontinued.

If moors and forests served to remind the poetic Elizabethans of their romantic past, monasteries and abbeys, even in their departing glory, suggested to them the recent religious changes, whilst the embattled walls and towering keeps of castles were at once a testimony to the old isolation of the nobles and the modern puissance of the sovereign. Scattered about the country were hundreds of conventual buildings. They had been erected in sheltered spots, with their moats and fishing-ponds, their gardens and woods. With their grey towers and sculptured windows they

KENILWORTH CASTLE.

broke the barrenness of hillside and moorland, or relieved the richness of plain and mead. The fat lands diligent monks had cultivated had passed into other hands. The rare windows of the abbeys were smashed, the roofs plundered of their lead, the stones used to mend the roads or build houses, the hospitiums were turned into barns. The castles were dotted all over the land. A list of the more famous would fill one of these pages. Some were in ruins, mementoes of the brigandage of early times; others remained, thrusting themselves above the house-tops of quaint towns, overlooking cliffs by the sea, frowning by placid rivers, piercing their way through embowering woods, and standing amidst their gardens and parks in all their magnificence and pride. In many of them stalwart nobles still lived surrounded by armed retainers, musing over their departed glories, when not engaged in the chase, or finding in effusive loyalty the cure for ambitious depression. Bolton, Tutbury, and Fotheringhay, will always be associated with Mary Queen of Scots; Kenilworth with the Earl of Leicester; and Sherborne with Sir Walter Raleigh.

The more commodious and pleasant houses of the nobility were in the valleys. They were generally in the enclosed parks, of which there were 4,000 "with timber fences," according to the Italian relation. It is impossible now to recover even their names. But they were pleasant places to live in, with their primeval oaks, under whose boughs hundreds of horsemen might shelter, with wild deer and fishing-ponds, heronries and falconries, mossy turf and choice cattle, with avenues and mazes, with handsome houses and wonderful Italian gardens. The castle had given place to the mansion, the mossy moor to the secluded park. There were Royal parks at Windsor, Shene, Nonsuch, Beaulieu, as well as in London. Fulbroke Park, or Charlecote, will ever be associated with the romantic part of Shakespeare's life, let dissolving research do what it may. Sir Thomas Lucy, "a Parliament man, a justice of peace," is supposed to be the original of Shallow in *The Merry Wives of Windsor.* John Thorpe, Bernard Adams, Lawrence Bradshaw, and Robert and Huntingdon Smithson, were the noted architects of the time. The palatial mansions in their glory at the end of the sixteenth century were Lord North's house at Catledge, in Cambridgeshire; the Marquis of Winchester's, at Basinghouse, Hunts; Sir T. Harrington's, at Kelston, Somerset; Sir N. Bacon's, at Gorhambury, Herts; Lord Buckhurst's, at Knowle, Kent; Sir H. Sidney's, at Penshurst, Kent; Lord Hunsdon's, at Hunsdon, Warwick; the Earl of Leicester's, at Wanstead; Lord Burleigh's, at Burleigh, Lincoln; Sir T. Gresham's, at Osterly, Middlesex; Sir J. Mynere's, at Longleat, Wilts; the Earl of Huntingdon's, at Stoke Pogis; Lord Cheyne's, at Toddington, Beds; Sir T. Cecil's, at Wimbledon, Surrey; the Countess of Shrewsbury's, Hardwicke, Derby; Wollaton Hall, Nottinghamshire; Haddon Hall, in Derbyshire. Domestic comfort was superseding feudal dominance, and embayed windows, castellated gateways, turrets, and twisted chimneys, built of warm red brick, were a pleasant contrast to the variegated scenery that grew about them. In the quadrangles were held brilliant pageants; at the embayed window the gay rhymer wrote his pastoral, or the daintily-ruffed lady read her Plato; on the terrace the moonbeams slept as gaily-dressed courtier and romantic maiden whispered their vows; in the dining-room, with its timber roof, its rows of armour, swords, and battle-axes, dark with blood-stains, the old soldier told his stories of wars in Ireland, the Netherlands, or the Welsh marches; by the massive fireplace in the ladies' room, with its piled logs and brass furniture, the ancient dowager sat in winter, whilst the wind lifted the tapestries, and hurried up the chimney, like a moaning, muttering spirit; in the park there was room for hawking and hunting, for tilts, and even for duels. Parts of the quadrangle, where there was only one, and the whole of a separate one where there were two, were taken up with kitchens, pantries, and storehouses. And then there was the garden, sometimes of many acres—a world of shady avenues, of espaliers, of clipped yews, of smooth lawns, of brilliant aviaries, of classic figures, of snug summer-houses, of ponds for goldfish, of cool and plashing fountains. "God Almighty first planted a garden," said Lord Bacon, with pious fervour; and when Laneham had seen the glories of Kenilworth, its fruits, flowers, birds, fishes, and trees, he said of it that, though it was "not so good as Paradise, for want of the fair rivers," yet it was "better a great deal by the lack of so unhappy a tree."

CHAPTER III.

TRADE AND COMMERCE.

English Wool and Corn—Coins—Merchant Adventurers and Foreign Trading Companies—English Woollens and Cloths—The New Trades Introduced by French and Flemish Immigrants—Coal and Metal Industries—Monopolies—The Pawn-banks.

"THE ribs of all the people throughout the world are kept warm by the fleeces of English wool." So wrote Matthew of Paris, compressing into a sentence a history and a picture. Prosaic writers who lamented the growth of pasture, as poetic souls mourned over the destruction of the woods, would lead us to believe that England had once been a great corn-growing country. Had it paid to cultivate corn, there would have been no breaking up of farms. The barley, rye, oats, and wheat, actually grown, sufficed for common wants, leaving a small margin for export from favourable districts. But the thinning of the people by plagues, wars, and a high death-rate, had as much to do with the increase of pasture as the greediness of the sheepmongers, of whose doings there were such fierce and pathetic complaints. The wool-trade had made what English prosperity there was. The agricultural population, dispossessed and driven into the towns, had, however, some real cause of complaint, as had the townsfolk whose commons were enclosed. The annual value of land was 1s. 4d.

to 1s. 8d. per acre in the period between 1536 and 1560, but about 6s. was the top price in the best counties at the end of the sixteenth century. The yield of wheat was not more than two and a half quarters per acre, though barley often produced four, and oats five quarters. Considering the richness of newly disafforested land, the wheat-yield was poor, but the preference seems to have been given to oats on the hilly lands where the forests had stood. Wheat fetched 6s. a quarter in Henry VIII.'s time, and its increase in price, till it reached 38s. at the end of the century, was due to various causes, amongst others the debasement of the coinage and the growth of luxury.

At the commencement of the century the shilling contained 114 grains of silver, but this had been reduced to 96 grains. The discovery of silver mines in America had lowered the price. Shakespeare refers by name to most of the coins in use, and also to the "slips," or base coins of silver-gilt brass, for making which convicted coiners were hanged. A large quantity of foreign money was in circulation. In 1561 all such coins except French and Flemish crowns, were called in to the Mint, out of whose issues the Queen had a royalty. York and some other towns had their own mints. The Easterlings, or Prussians, had introduced refining, and our word sterling is simply a corruption of Easterling. To retain as much gold and silver in the kingdom as possible, no strangers, who were not ambassadors or members of their suites, were allowed to carry out of the country above twenty crowns in cash.

Agricultural produce was brought for sale to such towns as had markets and fairs. Wool was conveyed to the staple towns of Newcastle, York, Lincoln, Winchester, Exeter, Bristol, and London. The merchant staplers re-sold it; they had their houses of business at Antwerp, Calais, and Bruges. But they were being superseded by the merchant adventurers, who did a more miscellaneous trade, and, chartered by royal licence, controlled all foreign trade not regulated by monopolists. Up to 1552, when it was dissolved, the London foreign trade was in the hands of the Steelyard Company, with their head-quarters in the Hanse towns of Germany, and affiliations in the English commercial cities. The London Companies were called liveries because they had a distinctive dress. Their despotic agents were at every port in the kingdom. At first only guilds, they gradually lost their associative character, and became societies of capitalists, appropriating the common funds, and keeping the poorer members in subjection.

Three great trading companies were formed in Elizabeth's time. The Company of New Trades was an association of freebooters, who sometimes committed serious depredations. The Company of Tripoli merchants was formed in 1579. William Harebone, Edward Ellis, and Richard Staple, visited Constantinople, and obtained from Amurath IV. the same privileges that other foreigners enjoyed. They imported from the East spices, perfumes, unwrought silks, tapestry, and indigo, briskly competing with the

Venice Company for the raisin trade of the Levant. In 1583 Harebone became our ambassador at the Sublime Porte. The third Company has a long and brilliant history. Greedy Dutch traders monopolised the Indian seas, and in 1599 they raised the price of pepper to England from 3s. to 6s. and 8s. in the pound. The Lord Mayor of London and others thereupon agreed to form a distinct Indian association, known at first as "The Company of Eastland Merchants." It received the royal charter in 1600. This was the origin of the East India Company. There was considerable conflict between the older London companies and these newly-formed associations.

The loss of Calais in 1558 deprived English merchants of several conveniences. Serious changes had set in, amidst popular laments. Several monarchs had tried to manufacture English wool at home by importing Flemish artisans. The cambric of Cambray, the calico of Calicut, the damask of Damascus, the dimity of Damietta, the diaper of Ypres, pottery from Delft, millinery from Milan, will still be recognised by the names they then bore. Flemings introduced the cloth trade in Yorkshire and the east and west of England. The woad-plant was still cultivated in the cloth regions for its dye. Lincoln green was famous, and so were the cloths of Kendal, Norwich, Peniston, and Halifax, as well as the coverlets of the city of York. Foreign uncertainties had caused the decay of these industries, and possibly the goods themselves were not as fine and as well made as those imported. Imperfect skill and bad materials would account for the roughness of the manufactured articles. "As we have the best wools in the world," said an old writer of the time, "so we ought to have the best cloths; but there is more false cloth made in this realm than in all Europe besides. All countries be trying to make their own cloths in consequence." As a matter of fact, this is what they had been doing for hundreds of years. The English cloth trade was new, and difficult to establish.

An effort to introduce kersey-making into Leicester had failed. Hose were made there. In 1594 Alderman Robert Herrick, apparently a relation of the poet, wrote to the Earl of Huntingdon in London: "I have sent up by Henry White, this bringer, forty pairs of good worsted hose, tied together in four bunches, which I pray you will sell for me for £12, or else lay them up in your press. I cannot afford them for less." In 1589 William Lee had invented the stocking-machine, but he had carried it with him to France, and hand-made stockings were the rule until some time after his workmen returned with the secret. In the early part of the century Coventry had been famous for its woollens and its dyed thread. "As true as Coventry blue" was a proverb. But the business had declined, though it was revived in the later years of the century, when the "tammies, camlets, and shalloons" of the city were staple articles of trade. There was a good market for Irish linen in some of the Cheshire and Lancashire towns. Chester, then known as West Chester. petitioned in 1566 for a cotton staple in the city. Coatings, or imitations in cotton of the worsted stuffs of the Continent, were made by the shermen, or drapers, cottoners, and pressers of Shrewsbury, and also at Bolton and at Manchester. The Manchester trade was yet in its infancy. Its fustians, vermilions, and dimities, did not become famous until the time of Charles I. The prevalent name of Walker is distinct evidence of a large Flemish settlement in Lancashire and Yorkshire. The fulling of cloths was effected by walking upon them, as may still be seen in the Hebrides, and the name of the fulling ground was the "walken milne."

When Cecil examined the condition of the kingdom in 1559, he was compelled to record for his own guidance that "those who depend on the making of cloths are of worse condition to be quietly governed than the husbandmen." Industry was much depressed, and towns were decaying. The religious struggles of the Continent soon came to the relief of Protestant England. Fugitives from France and Flanders, braving the sea in open boats, godly and simple men, looked with delight to the white cliffs and low shores of our southern and eastern coasts. From 1561 to 1568 the immigrants came steadily, "The foreign manufacturers," says Hasted, the Kent historian, "chose their situations with great judgment, distributing themselves with the Queen's licence throughout England, so as not to interfere too much with each other." At Sandwich they set up looms for the manufacture of bays, and London merchants flocked to the bi-weekly market. In 1582 there were 351 Flemish families in the town. Elizabeth protected them against local exactions. Children spinning fine bay yarn, "a thing well liked both of Her Majesty and the nobility and ladies," formed one of the special sights arranged for the Queen when she visited the town. Even in its present decay, Sandwich is quaint and Flemish.

In London the Flemings settled at Bermondsey, and engaged in joinery and felt-hat making. At Bow they established dye-works, at Wandsworth they made brass plates, at Mortlake arras, at Fulham tapestry. The Yorkshire Flemings had been driven out of Norwich, and so, in 1564, the Norwich people asked the Duke of Norfolk to obtain them more workmen. Dutch and Walloons were sent for, and bays, serges, silks, bombazines, and beaver-hats, were introduced there, and the town became the great manufacturing centre of England. When old jealousies revived, Elizabeth remonstrated against the unfair treatment of the poor men of the Dutch nation who had been "favourably and jintely received," and prayed them to mend their ways. Lace-makers from Alençon and Valenciennes settled at Cranfield, in Beds, in 1568, spreading their trade over the adjoining counties. The first bone lace at Honiton was worked with thread from Antwerp, by refugee Dutch, who have left their names in the lace towns of Devonshire. Foreigners were admitted to settle at Southampton, on condition of communicating certain arts and manufactures. As yet the factory system had not arisen, and no man was to possess more than two looms. The weaver did his work at home, and was no doubt often regarded with the same curiosity as the villagers eyed George Eliot's "Silas Marner."

Anthony Been and John Care began window-glass making in London in 1567. The windows of Wadham College, Oxford, and the fine window of Lincoln's Inn Chapel, were supplied by Bernard Von Linge, a Flemish glass-painter settled in London. Liège workmen introduced steel-making at Shotley Bridge, and workers in iron and steel were induced to settle at Sheffield by the Earl of Shrewsbury, and to instruct apprentices. In 1568 Dutch Protestants located at Yarmouth taught the people the art of curing herrings, which had formerly been done in Holland. Red or cured herrings were worth 3s. 4d. a hundred, and whilst Lent was strictly observed charitable persons left money to provide the poor with them. When Elizabeth stopped the Flemish trade, Sir Robert Killigrew opened negotiations with Hamburg to supersede Antwerp. A distinct record of the effect of these negotiations is supplied by the city of York. After the Reformation, St. William's Chapel on Ouse Bridge was converted into an exchange, where the Society of Hamburg merchants of York met daily for business.

The mining industries of the time were not extensive. The coal-trade was almost confined to Durham, Northumberland, and South Wales.

Newcastle coal was not in especial favour in London, and the brewers who used it in their furnaces, to the annoyance of the Queen, undertook, in 1578, to use wood in the breweries nearest to Westminster. Lead and tin were the staple products of Cornwall, as they had been for hundreds, perhaps thousands, of years. The roofs of the castles and churches of France were all made of English metal. The emigration of lead-workers had been forbidden. It had been reported to Elizabeth that precious metals might be found in Cumberland, and as no experienced English workers were to be had, in 1566 she negotiated for the introduction of German miners. John Stemberg received 500 crowns for sending the first contingent of twenty Germans to Keswick, to work the mines there. Gold was found on Crawford Muir, and Daniel Hechstether reported that he was surprised at the mineral riches in the district. Copper was also discovered at Newland. The Germans formed a small colony, though we have no information as to the ultimate extent of it, and they much wanted "a preacher in their own language." A few years later, when Frobisher brought home gold ore from the north-west parts, it was ordered to be placed in the Tower, "under four several locks and keys." German smelters were employed in testing it, and they furnished four proofs of assays in December, 1577. Some of the gold still attaches to the sealing-wax in the preserved documents. Mills and furnaces were erected at Dartford, and the interested adventurers were ordered to pay the cost. The later ore turned out badly. Alum was found in Yorkshire in 1609, at Robin Hood's Bay, where it is still worked, and its exportation was instantly forbidden.

The exercise of the royal power is seen in the granting of monopolies and the constant interference with trade. Orders, proclamations, licences, and grants, flutter forth like pigeons from a cote. The high price of grain in Cambridge market attracts the attention of the university authorities. It is complained to Cecil that such prices lead to "the pinching of poor scholars' bellies." Exportation from the district is at once stopped. Corn-badgers, as they are styled, are buying wheat on the Humber side. Their operations are speedily arrested by the withdrawal of the power of exportation from Kingston-on-Hull, then, as Drayton says, "newly-named Hull." A citizen of York, finding that more money was being put into the malt business than into other trades, as he believed to the detriment of the city, invokes, if there is no evidence that he obtains, the exercise of the royal authority. Certain Frenchmen ask Elizabeth to be allowed to import wine and woad to France, and the privilege is given in the face of a statute to the contrary. English noblemen wish to have wine duty-free, for their own consumption, and their prayer is granted, to the robbing of the revenue. Many prices are fixed by statute. Starch is freely employed for ruffs and collars, and somebody suggests that it affects the price of wheat. Out comes a royal proclamation, ordering that starch shall be made of bran, and only at certain places. Barley is scarce, when the remedy devised is a proclamation ordering the maltsters not to make their ale too strong, as by it barley is consumed that should be used for bread. If a man wants to travel in foreign parts, he must procure a licence. If he wishes to appeal to a generous public, he must obtain, as Thomas Norman, of Barnstaple, does in 1575, a licence "to collect alms in churches and towns, in consideration of his losses sustained at sea, and personal sickness." Even poor old Stow, the chronicler, has to come down to this low level, for on the 28th of February, 1604, as "a decayed citizen of London," he is granted a licence "for the collecting of men's benevolence."

The monopoly system, though it might be temporarily useful—as Adam Smith admits—could only keep up prices and restrain trade. Elizabeth granted all kinds of monopolies, even down to the exportation of old shoes. The trade in all the metals, in gunpowder, bottles, glass, coals, salt, hides, leather, horn, brandy, starch, wool, and other things, was controlled by companies or monopolists. A remonstrance by Parliament led her to cancel them; but there was a brisk revival of the evil under her successor. A reference to some of these monopolies will show the trade of the time. Sir John Hume was to export 1,000 dickers, or packages, of red hides, tanned, within two years; Lord Aubigny, to export 6,000 tons of double beer within six years; the Earl of Suffolk, a lease for the subsidy on currants for £500 a year; the Earl of Worcester, the sole making of saltpetre and gunpowder in England and Ireland for twenty-one years, "revocable at pleasure"; James Rhymer, the sole privilege of printing and selling certain Latin works of Hieronimus Zauchius for fourteen years, the price to be fixed by the Archbishop of Canterbury; John Speed, to print genealogies of the Irish scriptures, together with the maps of Canaan, for ten years; and Richard Penkewell, "to discover the passage into China, Cathay, the Moluccas, and other regions of the East Indies, for seven years." Court favourites received their rewards in monopolies, or by farming the revenue, at a large profit, when not by land grants.

The poverty of many common people, and the scarcity of money, led to a Bill, in 1571, for "the establishment of seven banks, to be kept in the cities of London, York, Norwich, Coventry, West Chester, Bristol, and Exeter, to be known by the name of the Banks for the Relief of Common Necessity, and to lend money on pledges, or pawns, at the rate of 6d. per cent." That a pretty good use was made of these pawn-banks may be gathered from Shakespeare, especially from the amusing scene between Falstaff and the Hostess Quickly, in *Henry IV.*, Part II. He is in debt to her, but he wants to borrow more money, and she replies that to raise it she must pawn her plate and tapestries. Sir John speaks to the point: "Glasses glasses, is the only drinking: and for thy walls, a pretty slight drollery, or the story of the Prodigal, or the German hunting in water-work, is worth a thousand of these bed-hangings and these fly-bitten tapestries. Let it be ten pound if thou canst." With a little protest this time, the Hostess declares, "You shall have it, though I pawn my gown." Such references must have been highly appreciated within twenty years of the introduction of the three gilded balls of Lombardy.

CHAPTER IV.

MARITIME DEVELOPMENT.

Royal Influence—The Fisheries—Privateering and Smuggling—The Viking Temper—Frobisher—Davis—Cavendish—The Hawkinses —Sir John Gilbert—Sir Francis Drake—Sir Walter Raleigh—Sir Richard Grenville—English Vitality.

IT is a disputed point as to how far royal influences improved English trade. We have seen how zealous Elizabeth was in the protection of foreigners who had many things to teach the English people. In other matters she was less wise. Her imposts seriously interfered with the shipping trade, which her father had endeavoured to develop. The duty on foreign wines, known as "the butlerage," arrested the brisk trade between England and France. "There's a whole merchant's venture of Bourdeaux stuff in him," said Doll Tearsheet of Falstaff, alluding to his paunch and his wine-bibbing. But fewer wine brigs had plied between France and England in consequence of the duties. Sir Peter Carew complained to Cecil that the wine-duties had destroyed the shipping trade of Dartmouth, and similar complaints were made from Hull, the great wine-port for the North. In the consumption of wine, however, no diminution was noticed ; it simply came in foreign vessels, leaving to English ships the trade in Eastern, New World, and Russian luxuries. An amusing list is given in the Domestic State Papers of some of these "unnecessary wares": Babies' dolls, valued at £178 3s. 4d.; tennis balls, at £1,699; cabbages and turnips, £157 16s. 8d.; cards, £2,837 10s.; fresh and salt eels, £1,580 13s. 4d.; and iron, £1,955 9s. 10d.

The change in the national religion had affected the fishing trade. In the summer the Iceland fleet had gone to the North for cod, ling, and sturgeon, supplying Normandy and Brittany as well as England. Frenchmen were now taking the trade. In the western seas, where Devonians and Cornishmen had trawled their nets, there was, as Cecil confessed, "a great navy of French within kenning of the English shores." The Irish fisheries were farmed by the Chester merchants, who did all the trade with Ireland. Liverpool was a poor port, with only 223 tons of shipping. Yet Drayton, with his quick eye, saw a great future for the river—

"Proud Mersey is so great in ent'ring of the main,
As he would make a show for empery to stand,
And wrest the thrice-forked mace from out grim Neptune's hand."

Cecil could discern but three remedies—an increase of merchants, more fishing, and "the exercise of piracy."

Measures to develop the second were taken, the third requiring no help. In the Parliament of 1562-3 an Act was passed making the eating of flesh on Fridays and Saturdays punishable by a fine of £3, or three months' imprisonment. Wednesday was to be a half fish day. Falstaff clearly refers to these regulations when he says that demure boys never "come to any proof," owing to cooling the blood with "thin drink," and "making many fish meals." The plague interrupted any virtue the orders might have immediately had, and it was some time before any improvement was noticed. Ten years afterwards, a great increase of shipping was noticed, other causes having been at work. James I. offered a bounty of five crowns a ton on all new ships.

Elizabeth winked at privateering, and was not prevented by any nice scruples from taking her share in a merchant's venture to the Indies, whether for legitimate or doubtful trade. During her reign the Killigrews, Carews, Tremaynes, Throgmortons, and other gentlemen adventurers, driven out of the country by the Marian persecutions, came back to scour the seas. The connection between Protestantism and piracy was once more visible. In the western counties, in the east, and the north, there was a strong inclination to downright plunder whenever a Flemish, French, or Spanish trader conveniently offered itself. Bold rovers rushed fiercely at mighty galleons, sweeping their decks with arrows, and plundering the cargo. Black luggers lay in waiting for ships that were never heard of again. Their treasures were hurried on shore, and stowed away in church towers and manor houses. Their crews were landed anywhere. The Spaniards served English ships in the same way, with this difference, that their crews were handed over to the Inquisition, which controlled all the Spanish ports. As was justly said, the Spaniards thought that by the hurt they could do to an Englishman they got heaven by it, and in turn the English rovers believed they advanced the cause of Protestantism. The French war increased the issue of letters of marque, and the attempts to suppress gentleman-piracy were either very feeble or they were not intended to succeed.

The old Viking temper did not restrict its range to European seas. In former ages Englishmen had tried to rescue the Holy Land from the dominion of the Crescent. It was now a contest with Spain for colonial empire and maritime supremacy. The sea-dogs of Devon, the ear-ringed mariners of Wapping, and titled adventurers from all parts, were romantically attracted by every fresh hint of the wealth of the Indies or the glories of the New World. They went forth in their small vessels as brave as lions. The *Squirrel* that bore Sir Humphrey Gilbert across the Atlantic was only of ten tons burden; Martin Frobisher's fleet, when he set out to discover the north-west passage to China, consisted of two 24-ton vessels and a pinnace of ten tons; and Sir Francis Drake circumnavigated the globe with five vessels, of which the largest was less than a hundred tons. The peril, the audacity, the determination of such sea-buffetings may well strike us with amazement, as it did the Spaniards. A sort of epic grandeur lingers about these wild voyages, spoiled by many cruelties, and desecrated by an iniquitous traffic in human flesh.

The great sea heroes of the time were Martin Frobisher, John Davis, Thomas Cavendish, Sir John

SHIPS OF ELIZABETH'S TIME—FROBISHER PASSING GREENWICH

Hawkins, Sir John Gilbert, Sir Francis Drake, Sir Walter Raleigh, and Sir Richard Grenville.

Frobisher was a native of Yorkshire, who made his first voyage to Guinea in 1554, and started in 1576, aided by the Earl of Warwick, to discover the north-west passage to Cathay. With three ships and thirty-five men, he sailed from Blackwall, with a God-speed from England's Queen. Deserted by one vessel, and having lost another, he reached Labrador, and finally the Bay named after him. The ore he brought back with him has already been referred to. His Cathay Company came to nothing. Next the Queen lent him the *Aid,* a ship of the Royal Navy, of 200 tons, and subscribed £1,000 as an adventure on his expedition. His old ships joined him, and his crews mustered 120 men. He took possession of the country about Hall's Island, naming it Meta Incognita. More black earth was found. The Queen received him graciously on his return, and he made a third voyage with a fleet of thirteen vessels. The Emperor of Russia claimed that the lands visited were part of his dominions. In 1585 he commanded the *Primrose* in Drake's expedition to the West Indies; in 1588 he was knighted for his exploits against the Armada; and in 1594 he received a wound at the siege of Crozan, near Brest, from which he died at Plymouth a few weeks later. The Queen commanded his remains to be buried in St. Giles's, Cripplegate.

John Davis was a native of Sandridge, near Dartmouth. In 1585, under the auspices of Elizabeth, he made his first voyage to discover the north-west passage to the Pacific. Passing round the southern corner of Greenland, he crossed the strait which bears his name, and penetrated as far as the Cape of God's Mercy, so named because he imagined his task was at end. A second voyage in 1586 yielded no fruits; but, in 1587, he penetrated to the strait subsequently explored by Hudson. A voyage to the South Seas led him to discover the Falkland Islands. On his third voyage to the East Indies he was killed by pirates, off the coast of Malacca. He published two or three accounts of his discoveries.

Thomas Cavendish was a courtier who took to the seas to repair his fortunes. He went to Virginia, in 1585, with Sir Richard Grenville, in a ship of his own, and the voyage so fired his imagination that he resolved on a grand buccaneering expedition. The next year he sailed from Plymouth with three ships, and performed some dashing exploits off the coast of Chili, Peru, and Mexico, burning or sinking nineteen ships, including the *Santa Anna*, a royal Spanish vessel, with a splendid cargo. He reached Plymouth in September, 1588, his journey round the world having taken him two years and fifty days. Plymouth Hoe was crowded with people to watch his return. His men were clad in silks, his sails were of damask, and his topmast ablaze with cloth of gold. A third voyage was attended with disasters that shortened his life. Port Desire, on the coast of Patagonia, was his most important discovery.

The Hawkinses were a race of seamen. William Hawkins, the father of the more famous Sir John, was an old Devon worthy, the pioneer of adventure in the Southern Seas, and, according to Hakluyt, "a man, for his wisdom, value, experience, and skill in sea causes, much esteemed and valued of King Henry VIII." His wife was one of the Trelawneys of Cornwall. John Hawkins, the son, and his brother William, were both trained to the sea. In extant despatches of Philip of Spain, where the name of John Hawkins occurs, "the sprawling asterisks in the margin," says Mr. Froude, "remain to evidence the emotion which it produced." He was the originator of the English slave-trade. His first venture in 1562 was not very successful, as he could not sell at St. Domingo all the negroes he took at Sierra Leone, "partly by the sword and partly by other means." He made sufficient profit, however, to induce Lord Pembroke and the Queen to join him in fitting out another expedition, consisting of two ships and two sloops. He swept up four hundred slaves on the African coast, disposing of them by stratagem, despite Philip's interdict. Spending the summer in the Caribbean Sea, he made his way home by the coast of Florida, and the banks of Newfoundland. The Queen, Lord Pembroke, and the other adventurers made 60 per cent. on their shares. Well might De Silva write to his master, Philip, that "the vast profit has excited other merchants to make similar expeditions." Philip trembled for his colonies.

Great preparations were made for a third voyage in 1567. Hawkins' object was "to lade negroes in Genoya (Guinea) and sell them in the West Indies, in trucke of gold, perles, and esmeraldes, whereof he doubted not but to bring home great abundance, to the contentation of her Highness, and the benefit of the whole realme." Elizabeth was alarmed at the vigorous remonstrances of Philip, but Hawkins did his best to pacify her. With five ships he slipped from Plymouth, in October, 1567. At Sierra Leone he founded an alliance with a negro tribe, sacked a town, crammed his ships with slaves, and then sailed for the West Indies. His ships and cargo were valued by him at £1,800,000. How he was driven by stress of weather into San Juan de Ulloa, how thirteen Spanish men-of-war subsequently entered, how he had to fight against land batteries and broadsides, how fire-ships were sent into his fleet, how fiercely he battled, how cleverly he escaped with two ships, how he reached Plymouth, how Sir Francis Drake, who had been with him, rode post-haste to London to tell the Queen that all his business had had "infelicity, misfortune, and an unhappy end," he has himself told us in quaint and graphic sentences that no modern sensational writer could surpass. The seizure of Philip's treasures at Plymouth and Southampton was Elizabeth's reprisal for the loss of this wealth. In the Armada fight Hawkins did splendid service. His son Richard had been made captive by the Spaniards off the coast of Quito in 1592, and three years later the father in vain attempted to rescue him. John Hawkins died, worn out with fatigue and failure, off Puerto Rico, November 12, 1595. A portrait of him was formerly visible in the Armada tapestry in the House of Lords.

Sir Humphrey Gilbert was another sturdy Devonian, with all a poet's love of blue water. Well educated, he was a favourite at Court, and served under Sir Philip Sidney in Ireland, and was for a time Governor of Munster. After fighting in the Netherlands he wrote a pamphlet on the North-west Passage, which Gascoigne published without his knowledge. No doubt it largely influenced Frobisher in selling his patrimony and collecting a fleet of eleven sail, manned by brave Devonians. Joined by his half-brother, Sir Walter Raleigh, Gilbert prepared to execute the Queen's letters patent, authorising him and his to discover and occupy such "heathen lands not actually possessed of any Christian prince or people as should seem good to him and them." A dispute at starting reduced his fleet to seven ships and 150 men, and with those he plunged into unknown seas in November, 1578, returning the next year, after some encounters with the Spaniards. In 1583 he got together another fleet, but the Queen would not let Raleigh accompany him. She sent him, however, a golden figure of an anchor, guarded by a lady, and wished him "as great good hap, and safety to his ship as if she herself were there in person." Two days after leaving Plymouth one of his ships deserted him. On the 5th of August he took possession of Newfoundland in the Queen's name. Voyaging southward a little later, he lost his largest vessel. The sequel is one of the romantic stories of the time. "On Monday, the 9th of September," according to the narrative of Captain Hayes, of the *Hind*, "the frigate was near cast away, but at that time recovered; and, giving forth signs of joy, the general, sitting aloft with a book in his hand (the Bible), cried out unto us in the *Hind*, 'We are as near to heaven by sea as by land.' The same Monday night the frigate's lights were suddenly out, and it was devoured and swallowed up by the sea." The *Squirrel* had gone down with as brave a sea-king as ever walked British oak. Longfellow has made Gilbert's death the subject of a beautiful poem. The fleet of ice of "the corsair Death" is made to bear down on the two English ships.

'His lordly ships of ice
  Glistened in the sun;
And on each side, like pennons wide,
  Flashing crystal streamlets run.
In the first watch of the night
  Without a signal's sound
Out of the sea, mysteriously
  The fleet of Death rose all around."

Sir Francis Drake was one of the lordly figures of the time. He embodied the daring and resolute elements of the national character. Educated by Hawkins, and apprenticed to a trader, he had seen much experience before, at twenty-two, he accompanied his half-brother in his ill-fated expedition as captain of the *Judith*. In 1570 he sailed to the Spanish main with a privateer's commission. Two years later, with three ships he captured the town of Nombre de Dios, crossed the Isthmus of Darien, obtained from a tree his first glimpse of the enchantments of the Pacific, and resolved "to sail an English ship in these seas." After burning several ships and plundering a mule-train of gold and silver, he returned home laden with spoils. A negro slave he had captured was presented to the Queen, and exhibited at Court as a curiosity. Elizabeth received her share of the booty. After volunteering with the fleet in Ireland, Drake prepared for the great expedition indissolubly associated with his name. His immediate object was to pass through the Straits of Magellan, into the south seas, which no English ship had yet ploughed with its keel. With five vessels and 166 men, he sailed from Plymouth, in November, 1577, virtually to invade the dominions of Spain. "He was now in the prime of his strength," as Mr. Froude describes him, "thirty years old, of middle height, with crisp brown hair, a broad high forehead, grey steady eyes, unusually long; small ears, tight to the head; the mouth and the chin slightly concealed by the moustache and beard, but hard, inflexible, and fierce. His dress, as appears in his portrait, is a loose, dark seaman's shirt, belted at the waist. About his neck is a plaited cord, with a ring attached to it, in which, as if the attitude were familiar, one of his fingers is slung, displaying a small, delicate, but long and sinewy hand. When at sea he wore a scarlet cap with a gold band, and was exacting in the respect with which he required to be treated by his crew."

The object of the expedition was kept as secret as possible, but Philip had been warned of its probable destination. The Cape de Verd Islands were visited and a few traders relieved of their goods. Brazil was reached, the Plate entered, and provisions ensured at St. Julian. The Straits of Magellan were passed, and Macao appointed as a rendezvous. The unknown seas were now explored; the *Pelican's* brass guns made sad havoc with many a lumbering galleon; bars of silver, chests of reals, and bales of silk, were captured; his vessels were enriched with pearls, emeralds, golden ornaments, and rare porcelain. Proceeding northward, he landed on the territory we now call California, named it New Albion, and refitted his ships. Thence he made the Moluccas, the Celebes, and Java, doubling the Cape, and reaching the coast of Guinea. On the 3rd of November, 1580, he entered the Sound amidst the greatest rejoicings, being the first Englishman who had ploughed a furrow round the world. He had been away two years and ten months. The delight of the Court and the people was unbounded. The Queen overwhelmed him with her congratulations. Ten thousand pounds were left in Drake's hands, "to be kept most secret to himself alone," and the remainder, consisting of twenty tons of silver bullion, five blocks of gold, eighteen inches long, and a quantity of pearls, emeralds, and other precious stones, was lodged in the Tower. His flagship, the *Pelican,* was brought round to the Thames, and beached at Deptford as a memento of his exploits. Another of his vessels, the *Golden Horn,* was also brought to the Thames, and of the sound timber that remained in his day Charles II. had a chair constructed, which he presented to the University of Oxford.

The Queen knighted her hero, and was continually seen walking with him, or talking to him. Burleigh foresaw trouble. Drake was restless. In 1581 he accompanied Hawkins to the Azores. In 1585 he obtained the Queen's assent to another Spanish expedition which was to injure Philip, and not compromise her. With twenty-five vessels, and Frobisher as one of his captains, he sailed for Vigo, where his presence created a panic; thence to Cape de Verd, where he missed the Indian fleet of Spain by a few hours, "the reason best known to God," as he said; to St. Domingo, the first city in the Indies, which he carried by assault, and then occupied, fining the inhabitants 25,000 ducats, and burning and plundering till it was paid; to Carthagena, the second city, ransomed for £30,000, in the same way; to St. Augustine, a port in Florida, on his way to Panama; and then homeward with yellow fever on board, and men dropping dead at their work. This aggressiveness of little England startled Spain and astonished Europe.

In 1587 Drake went to Lisbon, in command of thirty sail, six vessels belonging to the Crown, and the remainder equipped by merchant adventurers. Delaying letters were given him as he was about to start, forbidding him to enter any Spanish ports, or offer violence to its towns, or plunder its ships. But the plucky sea-dog had slipped his cables and was rounding Start Point. Vice-Admiral Burroughs, the controller of the navy, had been sent with him to proffer the timid counsels which so often stand for prudence. A shot at the *Lion*, on entering Cadiz, turned the timid Admiral back to sea. With his Devon and Wapping sailors, Drake passed on. A large galleon in the roads was sent to the bottom by a well-delivered broadside, and the Spaniards, panic-stricken, left their store-ships at his mercy. Rifled of their more available contents, they were sent adrift in flames to the town. Wine, corn, fruits, and oil, intended for the use of the Armada, were consumed in a mighty blaze. This was what Drake called 'singeing the King of Spain's beard." From Cadiz he came back to Cape St. Vincent, and thence he reached the Tagus, where he received orders from home to return. But he cleared the harbour of Corunna on his way. In two years he had done much to shatter the power of Spain. Off St. Michael he came across a splendid carack, or East Indiaman, whose treasures enriched the adventurers who had joined him as much for the hope of plunder as from motives of patriotism.

His later years were occupied in an unlucky expedition to place Don Antonio on the throne of Portugal, for which Elizabeth subscribed £6,000, and in West Indian adventures. In 1592 a splendid Spanish carack, the *Madre di Dios*, was captured by him off the Azores. It was 165 feet long, and had a crew of 600 men. The account of the disposal of its cargo will illustrate the business of merchant-adventuring. The vessel was laden with pepper, calicoes, linen, damask, taffetas, silks, and other Indian goods. The City of London purchased these contents for

£140,000, and then it was divided, one-third to the owners, to the company, and to the victuallers. The *Foresight*, one of the Queen's ships, was awarded £23,103 10s. 4½d.; the *Roebuck*, belonging to Sir Walter Raleigh, £20,422 3s. 10½d.; the *Dainty*, the property of Sir John Hawkins, £14,225 0s. 2½d.; the Earl of Cumberland's ships, £66,359 9s. 9½d.; and the ships belonging to the City of London, £15,889 15s. 9d. A few rich hauls like this speedily made men's fortunes.

Sir Walter Raleigh, in his time, played many parts. He was a scholar and a soldier, a courtier and a sailor, a poet and an historian. Like a true Devonian, he was ready for any exploit by land or sea. After volunteering to assist the French and the Dutch Protestants, he accompanied Sir Humphrey Gilbert to Newfoundland, campaigned in Ireland, was rewarded by an estate there, and is supposed to have won the Queen's favour by an act of gallantry celebrated in picture and song. In 1584 he fitted out an expedition to North America, and took possession of the territory still called Virginia, in honour of the Virgin Queen. The next year, with a fleet of twenty-one sail, he plundered St. Domingo and Carthagena, relieved Captain Lane, who was in distress at Virginia, and brought home the potato and the tobacco-plant. In 1589, he took part in the unsuccessful Don Antonio expedition. Again visiting Ireland, he made the acquaintance of the poet Spenser. In 1592 he accompanied the expedition to Panama. In 1595 he took possession of Guinea in the Queen's name, and subsequently obtained from James I. a patent for its settlement. He lost his son in an attack on the Spanish settlement of St. Thomas in 1618. His later fortunes were of a very chequered character, and he was eventually beheaded in one of the King's piques, for having made war against Spain. His "History of the World" and his minor writings all bear witness to his rare abilities. Complying with a suggestion he had himself made, Spenser addressed a letter to him explaining the purport of his "Fairy Queen." He is referred to by Spenser in "Colin Clout" as "the shepherd of the ocean." The second of the two mediæval fragments sung by Sir Hugh Evans, in the first scene of the third act of *The Merry Wives of Windsor*, is imperfectly given from Sir Walter Raleigh's "Nymph's Reply to the Shepherd."

But none of their deeds of daring excelled Sir Richard Grenville's exploit, as sung by Tennyson in his "Ballad of the Fleet." The *Revenge* and five other ships were met off the Azores by fifty-three Spanish vessels, some of enormous size. His comrades fled, leaving Sir Richard Grenville to the unequal combat:—

"And the sun went down, and the stars came out far over the summer
sea,
But never a moment ceased the fight of the one and the fifty-three.
Ship after ship, the whole night long, their high-built galleons came;
Ship after ship, the whole night long, with her battle-thunder and
flame;
Ship after ship, the whole night long, drew back with her dead and her
shame.

> For some were sunk, and many were shattered, and so could fight us no more—
> God of battles; was ever a battle like this in the world before?"

His men wounded, his ship riddled, his heart heavy, himself maimed, he still fought on until he could fight no more, and the Spaniards captured him and his. His magnanimous enemies praised him for his exploits:—

> "But he rose upon their deck and he cried:
> 'I have fought for Queen and Faith, like a valiant man and true,
> I have only done my duty, as a man is bound to do;
> With a joyful spirit, I, Sir Richard Grenville, die!'
> And he fell upon their decks, and he died."

The flag of England now floated in all seas. It was possible for Maria to say of Malvolio, in *Twelfth Night*, "he does his smile with more lines than there are in the new map of the augmentation of the Indies." Some voyagers had gone, as he remarks elsewhere, "to discover islands far away." Some were coarse traders, whose only thought was plunder. Others were gentlemen-adventurers, of knightly polish and religious fervour, who regarded the New World as a land of enchantments, who considered themselves the champions of a purer faith, and who did not forget their conceits and madrigals in the presence of untutored Indians and naked chiefs. The pale faces of Englishmen were seen on the canals of Venice and in the streets of Constantinople, in the towns of Hindostan and the isles of the Pacific, in the woods of Brazil and the swamps of Africa.

Their abounding vigour and vitality was the theme of the world. They must have found some other outlet if war and commerce had not combined with religion and national hate to impel them forth in search of El Dorado and the unknown isles and continents of the sea.

CHAPTER V.

GENERAL CHARACTERISTICS—ARMY AND NAVY.

Extravagance in Costume—Ladies' and Gentlemen's Attire—Cutting the Hair—Dress and Class—Manners—Duels and Street Rows—Life in Country Mansions—Food and Cooks—Few Vegetables in use—Consumption of Beer and Wine—Taking Tobacco—Domestic Interiors—Amusements and Sports—Archery—The Surveys and Musters—Imperfect Military Training—The Armada Enrolments—The Two Fleets—English Eagerness—Drake's Summary of the Fight with Spain.

WE seem to need the small-windowed rooms, the open roofs, the grey walls hung with armour or with tapestries, the rushes on the floor, and the solid furniture about us, to do justice to the brilliant costumes of the time. They were obviously devised for pictorial effect. The great feature was the constant change of dress. Plain Hollanders and austere Puritans never ceased to ridicule the gay mutability of the age. Even the Venetians, who set the fashion in so many things, were amazed at our gorgeous apparel—at the white and red crossed uniform of the London train-bands, at the gaudy liveries of men-servants and pages, at the laces and jewellery of the gallants, at the painted cheeks, the silks and velvets, of the ladies.

Queen Elizabeth set the fashion of extravagance, though she issued her proclamation against excessive apparel. She did not wear "the golden tresses of the dead," as Shakespeare says other ladies did, but she covered her head with feathers, with imitation serpent and other devices more fitting an American India than an English queen. Her dresses were excessivel gaudy, her jewellery was profuse, and she establishe the use of the hideous farthingale, or crinoline, some times wheel-shaped, at other times puffing out th dress like a half-filled balloon. Very open and lov dresses were common, frequently showing the whol of the breasts. Peaked stomachers were worn i several forms, but all unsightly, despite fine colours When the dress was tight about the figure, the sleeve were slashed and puffed out, and the waist adorne with a girdle, from which hung charms, a fan, or steel Venetian mirror. The ruffs about the neck, no unbecoming if small, were the theme of the fierces Puritan satire. Some were erect, like an open fa behind the head, propped up with pocking-sticks, o supertasses, as they were called. It is this ruff whic excites the vehemence of Stubbes, who stigmatise starch as an invention of the devil, to sustain hi "kingdom of great ruffes." The ruffs were tinted i various colours. Fans were made of gorgeous feather set in gold and silver handles. Long, open sleeve with their tails fastened at the shoulders, excite much satire. High-heeled shoes, or chopines, wer worn to give ladies higher stature. Hamlet refers t them, when he says to the boy-player in the Queen' part: "Your ladyship is nearer to heaven than whe I saw you last, by the altitude of a chopine." Frenc hoods, cauls of golden thread, and the peaked Mineve cap, were worn upon the head. Some of the indoo head-dresses are described by Falstaff, when he says to Mrs. Ford, "Thou hast the right arched bent of the brow that becomes the shiptire (a thing of sails and streamers), the tire valiant (a gold and peacock arrangement), or any tire of Venetian admittance." No wonder the ladies wished to be seen, and sat in the open doorways in the towns; or that a Parliament man, in 1614, in presenting a bill against extravagance in apparel, said, "Women carry manors and thousands of oak-trees on their backs." These foreign fashions did not escape Shakespeare's ridicule. The Duke of York, in *Richard II.*, complains that the king is too much engrossed with the

> "Report of fashions in proud Italy,
> Whose manners still our tardy apish nation
> Limps after, in base imitation.

The men were just as bad. Their doublets were of all colours and materials, peaked, puffed, and slashed. Their cloaks were of velvet, trimmed with lace, and fastened with golden clasps. Their hose were of silk and velveteen, bombasted out with wire into a semblance of the ladies' farthingale, or tucked under the doublet, French fashion, and puffed and gored about the hips. A Welshman's hose, that would fit anybody, were constantly ridiculed. When the puffed or trunk-hose came into vogue, the remainder of the leg-covering began to be called hose, and the upper part breeches. Gilded rapiers, shoes with silver buckles and rosettes, half-boots with fringes of lace, low-crowned hats with feathers and buckles, and high-peaked, or "copatain hats," as Vincentio calls them, in *The Taming of the Shrew*, with rings for the fingers and the ears, chains and ruffs for the neck, completed the array of the Elizabethan or Jacobean dandy. He was a composition of many parts. As Portia says of Falconbridge, the young baron of England, "He bought his doublet in Italy, his round hose in France, his bonnet in Germany, and his behaviour everywhere."

The dandy vied with the ladies in the free use of scents, dainty gloves, flowers, and trinkets. He touched and twirled his tufted mockadour, or handkerchief, in the most affected manner. He was exactly the being to hang a pastoral on a weeping willow, and to pen a sonnet to his mistress's eyebrow. As described by Jonson, he was a "mincing marmoset, made all of clothes and face," who dare not smile beyond a point, "for fear t'unstarch his look," and who had "travelled to make legs." Elizabeth managed to put down bombast breeches, and she classified dress, because the costly imitations of the less wealthy occasioned "the decay and lack of hospitality;" but she in vain attempted to stem the luxurious tendencies about her. She could shorten rapiers in the London streets, and she could restrain the middle classes. But her power was limited in other directions. One of the most curious bonds of the time shows her interference. Nicholas Revell, and eight other tailors of St. Martin's-le-Grand, bind themselves not to put more than one yard and three-quarters of kersey into any one pair of hose, and to cut the same "so as to lye close to the legges, and not loose or bolstred, as in auncyent tyme."

Stubbes and Lyly are much exercised about the cutting of the hair. The former represents the barber as asking "whether you will be cut to look terrible to your enemy, or amiable to your friends, grim and stern in countenance, or pleasant and demure." The moustache was "laid out from one cheek to another, yea, almost from one ear to another, and turned up like two horns to the forehead." "How will you be trimmed, sir?" asks a barber in Lyly's *Midas.* "Will you have your beard like a spade or a bodkin? A penthouse on your upper lip, or an alley on your chin? A low curl on your beard like a ball, or dangling locks, like a spaniel? Your moustache sharp at the ends, like shoemakers' awls, or hanging down to your mouth like goat's flakes? Your love-lock wreathed with a silken twist, or shaggy, to fall on your shoulders?" The love-lock was a long piece of hair under the left ear, usually tied at the end with a silk rose. Beards were dyed. Bottom mentions several tints:—"Your straw-colour beard, your orange-tawny beard, your purple-in-grain beard, or your French crown-colour beard." The beard of "formal cut," according to Jacques, denoted the justice of the peace, whilst the soldier was "bearded like the pard." The bristly untrimmed beard was rustic, but the tuft to pull at was the mark of the wit, the disciple of euphuism. In his capacity as Lord Chancellor of Cambridge, Burleigh put down excess of shirts and ruffs amongst the students, decreeing that "no scholar do wear any long locks of hair upon his head but that he be polled, after the manner of the gravest scholars, under the pain of six shillings and eightpence."

Dress denoted class. Apprentices were compelled by statute to wear round woollen caps, "plain statute caps," as Shakespeare calls them. Their doublets were to be of canvas, fustian, leather, or cloth, without ornaments; their stockings and hose of white, blue, or russet; their overcoats, in place of the short coat, of cloth, cotton, or baize; their shoes of unpinked hide, their girdles of leather, their ruffs plain, their only weapon the knife. The burgher or citizen nearly always armed with a short sword, wore a small ruff, had a gayer doublet, and was permitted to have a cloak, usually of a brown or chocolate cloth. Satin sleeves and doublets, with furred and scarlet gowns, of Venetian origin, and not suited, as an Italian said to "persons of quick temperament and eager fierce spirits," were marks of aldermanic dignity. Lawyers wore a loose black gown and a tight-fitting coif, or cap. Indeed, the wearing of black was restricted to law and divinity, the physician being permitted as much of the dandy's attire as his purse allowed. The yeomen dressed in homespun russet in the summer in frieze in the winter; the country gentleman in a brown or blue cloak, a plain doublet, and a featherless hat. The rustic was in grey, or "vile russetings;" the hind in a russet jacket, with red sleeves and a blue cap. Blue was worn by servants of noblemen yellow by those of bishops. Green was reserved for ladies' servants, or servants of men of high rank.

TOWN AND COUNTRY FOLK IN SHAKESPEARE'S TIME.

> "My men were clothéd all in green,
> And they did ever wait on thee;
> All this was gallant to be seen,
> And yet thou wouldest not love me,"

sings the author of "The Courtly Sonnet to Lady Greensleeves."

With men and women so "*point de vice* in accoutrements," manners were naturally precise and fantastic. Casa's "Galateo," a book of manners to which Lord Chesterfield was much indebted, and Castilio's "Cortigiano," a manual of elegance, were very devoutly studied. The "incredible courtesy," as an Italian styles it, of remaining uncovered, was largely practised in the presence of rank and beauty. Children of twelve were married in solemn state. All events in life were made the occasion of ceremony. Men went in procession everywhere.

Street quarrels were common between rival families and factions. The duel was the approved, though not a strictly legal, method of settling disputes. Fencing-schools, afterwards controlled by the local authorities, were in every city, and Salvolio's practice was taught in them. In *Romeo and Juliet* we have the tavern-swordsman described, who places his weapon on the table, saying, "'God send me no need of thee,' and by the operation of the second cup, draws it on the drawer, when indeed there is no need." Tybalt is described by Mercutio, in the same play, as follows:—"He fights as you sing prick-song, keeps time, distance, and proportion; rests me his minim rest, one, two, and the third in your bosom:

the very butcher of a silk button, a duellist, a duellist." When Ben Jonson had his duel with Gabriell, the actor, and killed him in Hogsden Fields, he was imprisoned, and "nearly at the gallows." The common people delighted in nothing so much as a little rough and tumble fighting. Their combativeness was especially noted by strangers, and it came out in very curious ways. To pelt a man in the pillory was a street-diversion that pleased boys as well as grown men; to join in the whipping of the beggars was eminently agreeable; to jeer at a butcher, who, mounted on horseback, with his face to the tail, and his bad meat carried before his eyes, was borne round the town, was fine sport; and even a good hanging served to gratify the destructive appetite which lies behind the fighting spirit.

There was more naturalness in the country mansions, where the ladies performed their household duties, studied Latin, and played on the virginals. The gentlemen amused themselves with hounds and hawks, with bowls and cards, read sonnets to the ladies, or capped verses and stories with the jester. Everybody rose early, and fasted till dinner-time, which was at half-past ten in the country, and twelve in the towns. Beverages, or "nuntions," were sometimes taken after dinner—in many country places, refreshment between breakfast and dinner is still called "nuntion"—but the rule was for two good meals a day, dinner and supper, both eaten in solemn silence. After dinner, or more generally after supper, the domestic fool made his appearance to divert the household. "Poor Yorick" was one of these "fellows of infinite jest." But the custom was dying out, because it was not easy to find men clever enough to play the part. Shakespeare alludes to this discontinuance in *As You Like It*, where it is said, "since the little wit that fools have was silenced, the little foolery that wise men have makes the greater show." Wolsey had had his faithful Patch, Sir Thomas More his Patterson, whilst Leicester had his William Kempe, and Queen Elizabeth her Tarleton.

An Englishman's appetite had always been famous. He was fond of good solid eating. The farmer always had his bacon and his flitches of salt mutton on hand, in addition to salt beef and barrelled herrings from Yarmouth. In all good houses there was an imposing array of salting-tubs. The art of stall-feeding was almost unknown, and fresh meat, if procurable in the winter, was very lean. It cost from a halfpenny to a penny per pound, which was equal to a penny or twopence of our money. Fresh fish was the luxury of the rich, obtained from their own ponds and streams. Salt fish was a common article of diet amongst the working classes. Rye and barley bread were eaten by the poor. Wheat was often three pounds a quarter, or, as we should say, 120s. The prices of bread and beer were regulated by local assize. Horsebread was the name given to bread conveyed in packs; manchet was a fine wheaten loaf of six ounces; mesline bread was the penny loaf; and mayn bread, or demain, was the same as that used in the sacrament. Cakes of oats and spice were on all good tables.

Pies and pasties were made of all sorts of things. Page invited Falstaff and his friends to a dinner of "hot venison pasty," wound up by "pippins and cheese." The fee farm rent of Norwich consisted of twenty-four herring pasties, of the new season fish, flavoured with ginger, pepper, cloves, galingals, and other spices. On one occasion King James I.'s servants complained that four instead of five herrings were in each pasty, and that they were "not baked in good and strong paste, as they ought to be." Artichokes were also baked in pies, with marrow, dates, ginger, and raisins. Pilchard pasties were a Cornish dainty. In fact, the various pasties still to be met with in Devon and Cornwall are representative "survivals" of Elizabethan diet.

The cooks were chiefly French, but a few of them were Italians. Harrison says they were "musicall;" Ben Jonson styles them "atheists." They caught the classic taste in their dishes; their confectionery often represented scenes from Homer or Ovid. Jonson describes the master cook as a professor, an engineer, a mathematician,

"——He designs, he draws,
He paints, he carves, he builds, he fortifies;
Makes citadels of curious fowl and fish;
Some he dry ditches, some moats round with broths;
Mounts marrow bones; cuts fifty-angled custards;
Rears bulwarks pies; and, for his outer works,
He raiseth ramparts of immortal crust."

Very few vegetables were used, and some were regularly imported and salted down. Cabbages and onions were sent from Holland to Hull. The Flemings commenced the first market gardens. Lettuce was served as a separate dish, and eaten at supper before meat. Capers were usually eaten boiled with oil and vinegar, as a salad. Eschalots were used to smear the plate before putting meat on it. Carrots had been introduced by the Flemings. Rhubarb, then called Patience, came from China about 1573. The common people ate turnip-leaves as a salad, and roasted the root in wood-ashes. Watercress was believed to restore the bloom to young ladies' cheeks. In fact, all vegetables were regarded more as medicines than as necessary articles of food. Flesh meals were more believed in than anything else. They were eaten with a knife and a napkin. "The laudable use of forks," as Ben Jonson has it, did not commence until 1611, and was rare for many years after. The custom came from Italy, and the first forks were preserved in glass cases as curiosities. A jewelled one was amongst the New Year's gifts to Queen Elizabeth.

Probably the absence of vegetables had something to do with the immense potations of the time. Iago said the English could beat all other nations, and were "most potent in potting." As tea did not come into England until 1610, and coffee until 1652, beer or wine was taken at all meals. The Queen would only take beer regularly. Her maids of honour breakfasted, or rather dined, off meat and beer. Single and double beers were on all tables. In the year 1570 the scholars of Trinity College, Cambridge, consumed 2,250 barrels of beer, as appears from the State papers of the time. Two tuns of wine a month were accredited to the suite of Mary Queen of Scots, during her confinement in England. "Few people keep wine in their houses," reported an Italian, "but buy it for the most part at a tavern ; and when they mean to drink a great deal, they go to the tavern, and this is done not only by the men, but by ladies of distinction." Of Spanish wines there were thirty-six kinds in use, and of French fifty-six. Falstaff preferred sack, or sherris-sack. It was sold at all taverns, and burnt sugar was stirred in it, as with claret and other wines, if not sweet enough for the palate. The proportion was a quarter of a pound of sugar to a quart of wine. We gather from Prince Henry's remark to Francis, the drawer, in *Henry IV.*, Part I., that pennyworths of sugar were sold to mix with a cup of sack. With his usual raciness, Falstaff exclaims, "If sack and sugar be a fault, God help the wicked!"

Tobacco-smoking was the latest fashion. Singular to say, there is not a single reference to the weed or to smoking in any of Shakespeare's works. Ben Jonson, however, makes copious references to it, and in uncomplimentary terms. Spenser makes Belphœbe gather "divine" tobacco to heal Timais. To teach the art of "taking tobacco," or tobacco-drinking, as it was sometimes called, making curls, blowing it down the nose, and other devices, seedy professors hung about the apothecaries' shops, where it was sold and smoked. The weed could be bought in country ıarkets, and Aubrey says the heaviest shillings were :lected, and purchasers received their weight in ind. King James issued in vain his famous 'ounterblast. Taylor, the water-poet, leaves it open › doubt whether the devil introduced tobacco in the rst coach or not; but the habit grew all the ame, until, in 1614, there were 7,000 vendors of 'irginia and Trinidado in London. The smoking 'ent on in shops, theatres, and even churches. The oach was coeval with the pipe. The Queen imported Dutch coach in 1564, the sight of which "put both orse and man into amazement," remarks Taylor. Some said it was a great crab-shell, brought out of :hina, and some imagined it to be one of the Pagan emples, in which the cannibals adored the devil."

Household arrangements reflected a somewhat ıxurious spirit. Gremio, describing his house to aptista, in the *Taming of the Shrew*, renders much etail on our part unnecessary:—

> "My house within the city
> Is richly furnished with plate and gold;
> Basins and ewers to lave her dainty hands;
> My hangings all of Tyrian tapestry;
> In ivory coffers I have stuffed my crowns,
> In cypress chests my arras counterpoints,
> Costly apparel, tents, and canopies,
> Fine linen, Turkish cushions bossed with pearl,
> Valance of Venice gold in needlework,
> Pewter and brass, and all things that belong
> To house or house-keeping."

'ictures on the walls were veiled, and so were statues ı niches. Silver drinking-cups and dishes, rich chimney-pieces, handsome beds and quilts, Venice mirrors, carved oaken presses, china and glass, were to be seen in all good houses. Glass windows were getting so common, as Bacon said, that "we cannot tell where to come to be out of the sun or the cold." Three things had been marvellously altered in Harrison's time. First, "the multitude of chimneys lately erected," whereas formerly "each one made his fire against the reredosse in the hall, where he dined and dressed his meat;" secondly, "the great amendment of lodging," in the substitution of feather-beds and pillows for straw mattresses and wooden bolsters; and thirdly, "the exchange of vessels, as of treen (wooden) platters into pewter, and wooden spoons into silver or tin."

The indoor amusements were cards, draughts, dice, and dancing. Cards were very extensively played in all ranks of society. The dances were of many kinds. The brawl was a joined hands arrangement, the partners kissing each other. Elizabeth was fond of this dance, and hence Gray's lines with reference to Stoke Pogis:

"Full oft within the spacious walls,
When he had fifty winters o'er him,
My grave Lord Keeper led the brawls;
The seals and maces danced before him.

"His bushy beard and shoe-strings green,
His high-crowned hat and satin doublet,
Moved the stout heart of England's Queen,
Though Pope and Spaniard could not trouble it."

A few other dances may be briefly described. The

pavin, or pavan, from *pavo*, a peacock, was a grave and majestic dance, in which the gentlemen wore their caps, swords, and mantles, and the ladies their long robes and trains. The dancers stepped round the room and then crossed in the middle, trailing their garments on the ground, "the motion whereof," says Sir J. Hawkins, "resembled that of a peacock's tail." The slow step used in crossing the room was called the "cinque-pace;" and Shakespeare makes Beatrice, in *Much Ado About Nothing*, contrast it with livelier dances, to illustrate wooing, wedding, and repenting. "The first suit is hot and hasty, like a Scotch jig, and full as fantastical; the wedding, mannerly-modest, as a measure, full of state and ancientry; and then comes repentance and, with his bad legs, falls into the cinque-pace faster and faster, till he sinks into his grave." In the canary dance the gentleman led the lady to the end of the hall, retreated and then advanced; he then went to the other end, and waited there whilst the lady observed the same motions. Lafeu, in *All's Well that Ends Well*, referring to lady-influence, says he has seen a medicine that will

> "——make you dance canary
> With spritely fire and motion."

To "canary it," as Moth advises Armado, was to be lively on the feet.

But the outdoor pastimes were more popular. Castles, halls, and mansions, were too small to contain the meat-eating, beer and wine-drinking spirits of the time. Fierce sports in the open air delighted them most. Elizabeth loved bear- and bull-baiting in public, and amused herself with performing apes in private. James I. had a fine taste for fighting cocks, and kept many varieties, with a high-salaried and most fortunate gentleman, called his "cockmaster." Throwing at cocks with a stick was a Shrove Tuesday game. The cock was supposed to be a kind of devil's messenger, from his crowing after Peter's denial. Hence many divines enjoyed cock-throwing as a pious exercise. Hawking with foreign birds, and hunting the deer, were week-day sports. But the common people played at football, held fairs, and otherwise kept a most unholy Sabbath, whereat Stubbes, in his "Anatomy of Abuses," is mightily wroth, not without good cause. The church-ales, in which God's house was turned into a drinking-shop for profit, the ale having been brewed by the churchwardens for sale, led to abominable orgies. Tilting at the ring was another popular amusement for such as rode horses. Jousts and tournaments were always held as parts of the Royal progresses, and proclamations were issued, summoning "lusty knights to show feats of arms." The various ceremonies connected with May-day, fiercely attacked by the Puritans, were falling into desuetude. They had been frequently associated with much immorality.

Shooting at deer with a cross-bow was an amusement of great ladies. Buildings with flat roofs, called stands, partly concealed by bushes, were erected in the parks for the purpose. Hence the following dialogue in *Love's Labour's Lost*:—

BEAR-BAITING AS PRACTISED IN THE TIME OF QUEEN ELIZABETH.

Princess. Then, forester, my friend, where is the bush
That we must stand and play the murderer in?

Forester. Hereby, upon the edge of yonder coppice;
A stand where you may make the fairest shoot.

Great efforts were made by Elizabeth to preserve the use of the long-bow, declared by Ascham to be "the most honest pastime in peace," and "a most-sure weapon in war." Each town had two turf-butts for constant practice. The arrows were of ash, the heavier ones for use at two hundred and fifty yards, the lighter ones for longer distances. In length they were from two and a half to four feet. It would take a very strong arm and wrist to send the heavy arrow two hundred and fifty yards, and no one could do it now without careful training. The power to do so had failed in the later French wars, and our archers were reviled as their arrows fell short. The Bowyers, Stringers, and Fletchers of to-day are descendants of the bow and arrow makers of the ages before guns and rifles. The people were getting tired of archery, however, and, as Stowe says, "bows were turned into bowls." Bowls were made an unlawful game, and commissioners were sent into the country to search out and punish persons who permitted or indulged in them, but without much effect. In 1599 bows finally disappeared from the muster-rolls. In 1621 it was moved in Parliament that the old archery regulations should be repealed, as "guns be now the service of the State, and long-bows obsolete."

There was no standing army, so it was important to connect pastimes with military training, and to make careful preparations long before war actually commenced. For the eight years previous to the sailing of the Armada, in July, 1588, there had been the bustle of extensive preparations. Commissioners had surveyed all the creeks and bays around the coast, with the little forts and block-houses, the castles and towers, that defended exposed points. Instructions had been issued for the breeding and training of horses, and many fine animals roamed the parks of the nobles, or were confined in the paddocks of the yeomen. Special commissions had been addressed to leading noblemen of the country, ordering them to prepare complete musters of all men available for fighting purposes. The assembling of such men once in every three years had been the rule, but it had not been very strictly carried out. For example, one Captain Edward Turnour wrote to Cecil from Portsmouth, in 1559, where he said he was living like a conjurer amongst devils, and complained that "the sacred profession of perfect men of war is now by ill-training grown to misorder and mischief." It is certain that the militia were imperfectly cared for until Spain became menacing. It seems, however, clear that too much stress has been laid on the general neglect of Elizabeth, and those about her, to provide for an emergency that might arrive at any moment.

But directly danger was threatened strict instructions were issued for internal defence. The beacons were put in order; light horsemen, or hoblers, were attached to each district to fire them when news arrived, and to convey the intelligence to points where

SOLDIERS OF THE TUDOR PERIOD.

there were breaks in these fire-signals; wood and tar were kept in readiness. The militia knew where to muster when the beacon blazed on tower and hill. Town armouries existed, where guns and pikes, bows and arrows, and all the implements of war, were stored. Some of the musters show a considerable density of population, whilst in others we find indications of small towns of considerable poverty. The county of Derby could only turn out 660 able men, and Nottingham, complaining of its poverty, mustered but 2,000. Cornwall, where archery had not been suffered to decline, returned a roll of 4,000 able men. But the big musters were nearer London. Norfolk returned a list of 9,260 fighting men; Suffolk, of 10,749; Kent, of 12,131; and Essex of 13,362.

In dress and weapons the national array exhibited a picturesque variety. Armour had not yet gone out, but it was less cumbrous and rigid. The corselet, with a *morion*, or open head-piece, and *tassets*, or thigh-guards, were still in pretty general use; but plates of armour were frequently fastened to any ordinary tunic for the defence of the shoulders, arms, and chest. Skirts of mail were much in vogue, and the suits of wealthy officers blazed with plated ornaments, of little use in rough fighting. The pike-men, with their twenty-foot pikes, wore corselets, and were much disinclined to march more than five or six miles a day, owing to the weight of their dresses and weapons. The bill-men were in lighter armour, and their weapons were shorter than the pike, but very effective against cavalry. The bill was a hook-shaped blade fastened to a wooden staff, with a projecti prong at the end and back. Pike-men and bill-m were employed in protecting archers from cavalr and in covering such field-guns as were in use. Civ guards and watchmen were armed with bills, and hen Dogberry's caution to the watch, "have a care th your bills be not stolen." The archers usually di charged their long arrows from behind the ranks the pike-men and bill-men. They wore a buff-padde jacket, with sometimes an under-shirt of light chai armour. The mounted troops were armed with dem suits of plate, although a rusty cuirass was sometim turned out of a castle armoury. A jerkin, or sho jacket of leather or cloth, was indiscriminately wor by all ranks. In fact, the town armouries would hav supplied much excellent stage-furniture. It may b doubted whether some of their contents were of an other value.

The firearms were of two kinds, leaving out view artillery, as the term is now understood. Th first could be fired without a rest, and the second wer practically very light artillery. The *harquebus* an the small *petronel* belonged to the first class, and th *culverin*, the long *petronel*, and the *muschite* (from th French *mousquet*, a hawk) to the second. Two me were required to handle the weapons of the secon class. They had heavy, long barrels, and no stocl They were fired with a match, the barrels resting o an iron fork sticking in the ground. The petronel wa used by the cavalry, and the name subsequently serve to indicate a swaggerer. Mounted men so armed wer alled "shot on horseback." The harquebus was riginally a musket-stock with a bow fixed to it; but he term was now used to mean the long-barrelled and-gun, with a touch-hole and priming-pan and rigger on the right side, which was rapidly driving ut other weapons and rendering armour useless. Its ntroduction had much to do with the complaints oncerning Elizabeth's parsimony, which was un-doubtedly great, and her negligence, which is not very learly proved. More time was required for training nen in its use, and complaints to that effect poured n from several counties. They needed patience, too, or the harquebus required several minutes to fire. Special regiments were armed with this weapon, or and-gun, as it was more frequently called, and they vere then styled "shot."

Suggestions for increasing the number of mounted nen, for providing officers, for better training, and ven for a kind of mitrailleuse, which was to dis-charge twenty-four bullets at a time, are to be found n the Domestic State Papers. There was consider-able difficulty about officers, as the nobility and their ons usually led the county militia, and many of hem had wasted their youth in the gay pleasures of London, or preferred the writing of sonnets to the drilling of rustics. Yet, when war was announced, he country people were more eager to serve as the rivate servants of the local nobility than in the anks amongst the common soldiers. The rank and le were very ignorant. The choice men of Cheshire nd Lancashire had only been trained one day a year instead of six; and London, with a population of 150,000, could only turn out 10,000 fit men; her captains, however, had been well exercised in the Artillery Gardens.

The spirit of the men was undoubted. Some of them had displayed their stoutness in Ireland, in the Netherlands, and in France. They were eager to communicate their skill to others. When they met, county by county, it was hard to catch the words of command, so pronounced were the different dialects. But a common aim and purpose animated them all, and they mustered and marched with an eagerness and a courage that would have helped them against the better-drilled and better-armed regiments of Spain. The Duke of Parma, who was to bring over his fighting men from the Low Countries, evidently did not expect an easy victory. "England has made great preparations," he wrote to Philip, and as she could not be surprised, instead of 30,000 men "50,000 would be few." "For," he said, "when I shall have landed I must fight battle after battle." An insurrection of Catholics in London and elsewhere was relied upon as much as anything, and, to prevent it, care had been taken to keep arms out of the hands of such as were known to be doubtful, and to maintain a strict watch over them. The army enrolled to defend England in the summer of 1588 was estimated at 86,016 foot and 13,831 cavalry. Of this number 48,000 were pretty fairly trained in ordinary exercises and the use of the long-bow and the harquebus. The honour of defending the Queen's person was to be entrusted to the stout-hearted men of the midland counties, under the Lord Chamberlain Hunsdon ; and Leicester was to be commander-in-chief, with thirty or forty thousand men, to interpose between the enemy and London. The coast musters were to fall back before the enemy, and a reserve of 20,000 men was to prepare for a possible diversion in Hampshire.

The Spaniards were more afraid of us on sea than on land, and with good reason. Drake had singed Philip's beard, and our privateers had performed deeds that made them tremble to recount. At three or four to one they felt themselves barely a match for English captains and English seamen. But our fleet proper was as badly off as the army. The dockyards had been starved, the provisions were scanty, the ammunition short, the ships small, the men, though well trained, not too abundant. In Sir John Hawkins, the complete seaman, however, Elizabeth had a host. She made him head of the navy, and he did his work well, turning out his ships in splendid condition, as far as his care and forethought could avail. The navy numbered thirty-four vessels, from 1,100 to 30 tons, carrying 837 guns and 6,279 men. The City of London equipped 30 ships, and Southampton, Poole, Dartmouth, Plymouth, Barnstaple, Bristol, and other places, sent their brigs and barques. When the final tussle came England mustered 197 ships, of an aggregate tonnage of 29,744 tons, manned by 15,785 seamen. With this force she was ready and eager to do battle with the Armada Spain had been preparing for years, under the blessing of the Pope and with the spoils of the Indies. The Armada—it is never too stale to recount—consisted of 130 ships, in ten squadrons, of a total tonnage of 59,120, with 3,165 guns, 19,295 soldiers, 8,252 sailors, and 2,088 galley-slaves, besides illustrious volunteers numbering at least 2,000 men. Alexander Farnese, Duke of Parma, was to join the armament in Calais Roads with 17,000 soldiers, and then, taking the supreme command, to land at Margate, and march direct to London.

For months before the great expedition set sail there had been intense excitement in England. The fleet was ready in January, and was then dispersed by the Queen's orders. Drake had been wasting money, as she thought, in target practice. The Queen herself was wasting time, as all knew well, in negotiating a treaty. This "uncertain dallying" angered Sir John Hawkins. Howard, the Lord Admiral, protested that if Spain were to come upon us suddenly she would find us "like bears tied to stakes." Early in May the prospect of peace was at an end, and the fleet was once more got ready. Provisions were issued to the middle of June; but they did not arrive at the western ports, and, when they did the biscuits were weevilled and the beer sour. The sailors at Plymouth were praying either for the enemy or the victuallers. The Queen herself was inclined to be niggardly and merry, whilst her seamen were on short commons, and wild winds tossed them about in Plymouth Sound, without damping their courage, or straining their stout ships. At the beginning of July Drake actually made an attempt to reach Spain, and see what was going on;

but he returned to the Sound, fearing the enemy might give him the slip.

At last the Armada sailed, but only to meet a terrible doom, most graphically described in the pages of Mr. Motley and Mr. Froude. Sir Francis Drake's account of the matter is very pithy and quaint. "Beaten and shuffled together from the Lizard to Calais, driven with squibs from their anchors, and chased out of sight of England about Scotland and Ireland, their invincible and dreadful navy, with all its great and terrible ostentation, did not in all their sailing about England so much as sink or take one ship, bark, pinnace, or cock-boat of ours, or even burn so much as one sheepcote on this land." Whether as much success would have attended our Shakespearean Englanders had the fight been on land as well, is one of those speculative questions which fascinate but cannot be solved. Mr. Halliwell Phillips thinks it probable that Shakespeare himself wrote a ballad about the Armada fight, which has been lost. His audiences, however, would not miss the purport of the fine lines he put into the mouth of the Bastard, in *King John:*—

> "This England never did nor never shall
> Lie at the proud foot of a conqueror."

CHAPTER VI.

RELIGION AND EDUCATION.

Legal Establishment of Protestantism—New Hopes—The Condition of Churches and Parishes—Gradual and Imperfect Changes—The Catholic Party—Preaching and Prophesying—Psalms and Surplices—Introduction of Pews—Puritanism—The New Poor Law—Universities and Grammar Schools—Education and Travel—Ignorance of the Common People.

PROTESTANTISM had been finally established as the national religion the year before Shakespeare was born. Hence, from his earliest days, he would be familiar with its rites and ceremonies. The images would have been torn from the church by the gentle river Avon, and the fires of the Marian martyrdom, as well as the burning of Marys and Johns, would be memories of the past. John Fox, the author of the "Acts and Monuments," had published the first volume of his history before the poet's birth, and he had been tutor to the children of Sir Thomas Lucy of Charlecote.

The accession of Elizabeth, November 17, 1558, had lifted a dark cloud from the country. Bells rang, bonfires lit up the sky, imprisoned priests and people experienced the throbbing of a new hope, and far-off exiles gathered themselves together to take ship for their old homes, bringing with them the leaven of the Genevan theology. More anticipations were indulged than could ever be realised. The picture of the time has all the light and darkness of a work of Rembrandt. The Protestants were strong in the large towns and the seaports, but, in the north, the ennobled families were nearly all Catholics, though the common people had espoused the cause of England against the encroachments of Rome.

Many churches were closed, and there were hundreds of parishes without incumbents, devoting the Sunday to sports and licentiousness. The windows of the sacred edifices were broken, the doors were unhinged, the walls in decay, the very roofs stripped of their lead. "The Book of God," says Stubbes, "was rent, ragged, and all be-torn." Aisles, naves, and chancels, were used for stabling horses. Armed men met in the churchyard, and wrangled, or shot pigeons with hand-guns. Pedlars sold their wares in the church porches during service. Morrice-dancers excited inattention and wantonness by their presence in costume, so as to be ready for the frolics which generally followed prayers. "Many there are," said Sandys, preaching before Elizabeth even after her reforms, "that hear not a sermon in seven years, I might say in seventeen." Several towns and cities were notoriously irreligious. In the city of York, according to Drake, the Reformation "went so far as almost to put an end to religion."

The friends of the new doctrine expected that all the evils of the time would be instantly remedied. But the work of reform was extremely gradual. Until a month after her accession, Elizabeth did not interfere. Camden has pithily described the successive steps :—

"The 27th of December it was tolerated to have the Epistles and Gospels, the Ten Commandments, the Symbols, the Litany, and the Lord's Prayer, in the vulgar tongue. The 22nd of March, the Parliament being assembled, the order of Edward VI. was re-established, and by Act of the same the whole use of the Lord's Supper granted under both kinds. The 24th of June, by the authority of that which concerned the uniformity of public prayers and the administration of the Sacrament, the Sacrifice of the Mass was abolished, and the Liturgy in the English tongue more and more established. In the month of July the Oath of Allegiance was proposed to the Bishops and other persons ; and in August images were thrown out of the temples and churches, and broken or burnt."

The fervour of the last part, carried out by the common people, filled the streets with bonfires and crowds. The proceedings in London are described as being "like the sacking of some hostile city." Vestments, Popish Bibles and books, ornaments, and rood-screens, were ruthlessly destroyed. The Articles, revised and reduced from forty-two to thirty-nine, the changes in them being chiefly of a Lutheran character, were sanctioned and published in 1563.

The dispossessed Catholics strove to regain their place and power by resorting to artifice and intrigue. Some remained in England sheltered in the houses of the nobles. Others fled the country, taking the pay of the monarchs who were hostile to England. The charms of a freebooter's life on the open seas overcame others. The more desperate plotted against Elizabeth's person, or for the elevation of Mary Queen of Scots to the English throne, even taking arms, as in Northumberland and Yorkshire, for her cause. Elizabeth herself wavered. She was fond of an imposing ritual. Though she had been persecuted for her faith, she still leaned more to Rome than to Geneva. She restored the Carnival. At times it seemed as if little were required to make her a Catholic after the Pope's own heart. One of the matters which troubled her greatly was the marriage of the clergy. On her visit into Essex and Suffolk she found many of them had availed themselves of the altered law, and had given up celibacy. Accordingly she issued her injunction to Archbishop Parker against the marriages of deans and canons. Mr. Froude's picture of cathedral establishments is worth giving :—

> "Deans and canons, by the rules of their foundations, were directed to dine and keep hospitality in their common hall. Those among them who had married broke up into their separate houses, where, in spite of Elizabeth, they maintained their families. The unmarried 'tabled abroad at the ale-houses.' The singing men of the choir became the prebend's private servants, 'having the Church stipend for their wages.' The cathedral plate adorned the prebendal sideboards and dinner-tables. The organ-pipes were melted into dishes for their kitchens; the organ-frames were carved into bedsteads, where the wives reposed beside their reverend lords; while the copes and vestments were coveted for their gilded embroidery, and were slit into gowns and bodices. Having children to provide for, and only a life-interest in their revenues, the chapter, like the bishops, cut down their woods, and worked their fines, their leases, their escheats and wardships, for the benefit of their own generation. Sharing their annual plunder, they ate and drank and enjoyed themselves while their opportunity remained; for the times were dangerous, 'and none could tell who should be after them.'"

The Protestant party was growing in strength, but the Queen manifested her dislike of their proceedings, at times, in a very irritating manner. It was considered, disorderly for any State affairs to be mentioned from the pulpit. Subservient archbishops and bishops were instructed to admonish any clerks daring enough to discuss ecclesiastical changes and necessities. When Dean Nowell was preaching before Elizabeth at St. Paul's he rather "roughly handled" so un-Protestant a subject as images. The Queen got excited, and cried out from her seat, "To your text, Mr. Dean! Leave that; we have heard enough of that! To your subject." Of course the preacher was unable to proceed. The Queen and De Silva, the Spanish Ambassador, left in a hurry, and some of the Protestants present burst into tears.

In the southern churches the Protestant clergy held informal meetings for a service, in which preaching was the prominent feature. These meetings were known as "prophesyings," and afterwards as "Grindalisings," because Archbishop Grindal had encouraged them in the north, and, when promoted to Canterbury, had addressed a remonstrance to the Queen on the subject, against her wish to cut down the number of preachers. For his freedom Grindal was sequestrated. "We admit no man to the office," he had said, "that either professeth Papistry or Puritanism. Generally the graduates of the Universities are only admitted to be preachers, unless it be some few which have excellent gifts of knowledge in the Scriptures, joined with good utterance and godly persuasion." In vain he assured her that they were loyal subjects, and that in the Catholic rebellion in the north "one poor parish in Yorkshire, which, by continual preaching, had been better instructed than the rest—Halifax, I mean—was ready to bring three or four thousand men into the field to serve against the said rebels." The prophesiers, sometimes termed lecturers, had to be restrained, as their sermons were often three hours in length. Modern statesmen would have judged it prudent to leave them liberty to weary out their hearers and themselves. But, as it was, when the preacher turned his hour-glass, saying, "one glass more," the people murmured their delight, such was the eagerness of many of them to receive spiritual edification. There were objections, however, and worldly-wise Selden states them. "They ran away with the affections of the people, as well as with the bounty that should be bestowed on the minister."

Preaching at St. Paul's Cross in London was carefully regulated. When not a Londoner, the preacher was lodged in the Shunamites' House hard by. It was at this house that Richard Hooker asked the lady to find him a wife, and Mrs. Churchman successfully recommended her daughter Joan, whose peculiarities afterwards tortured the "judicious" mind of her husband, without preventing him from writing his exposition of ecclesiastical polity.

The services in the church were indeed uniform in certain externals, but they varied greatly, according to the amount of Protestantism in the bishop of the diocese, or the incumbent of the parish. Congregational singing was one of the conspicuous changes made by the reform-movement. Psalm-singing and heresy were both supposed to be of foreign origin. Free living and free thinking were common in Italy, and hence to be "Italianate," or "Italionated," was equivalent to being styled an atheist, a republican, or a worldling. To sing psalms was to be strongly Lutheran, but not Puritanic. According to Neale, the Puritans allowed congregational singing in a plain tune, but not of "tossing the psalms from one side to another, with intermingling of organs." Time and tune seem to have made the difference between the two schools of song. The Puritans drawled their tunes and psalms, Geneva-fashion; the Protestants sang them in a lively and tossing style. The clown in the *Winter's Tale* was thus speaking ironically when he says of the singers coming to the sheep-shearing feast, "but one Puritan amongst them, and he sings psalms to hornpipes." The other Shakesperean reference to the services of the time is also put into the mouth of this privileged character. "Though honesty be no Puritan," says the clown to the Countess of Rousillon, in *All's Well that Ends Well*, "it will wear the surplice of humility over the black gown of a big heart." Considering how freely he touched the life of his time, it augurs either absolute indifference, or calm neutrality, on his part, that so little was said by Shakespeare that could be considered offensive to reasonable hearers, or that can now be tortured by sectaries into proof of his special leaning and faith. Besides the references just given two others may be quoted, if single passages mean anything. "I'll have thee burned," says Leontes to

Paulina, in the *Winter's Tale*, one of his latest plays. She replies—

> "I care not.
> It is an heretic that makes the fire,
> Not she which burns in it."

On the opposite side there is a slap at the Norwich divine, when Sir Andrew Aguecheek confesses, in *Twelfth Night*, he would "as lief be a Brownist as a politician."

Pews did not make their appearance in the parish churches until the reign of James I. They were then stuck about immediately under the pulpit, or anywhere, as may still be seen in some out-of-the-way village churches. The pews were of oak, and they were built in the first instance by the families sitting in them. "The faculty pew," intended for the medical men for the time being, appears, in one or two instances we have noticed, to have been constructed at the expense of the parish. Green baize from Norwich was used to line them, and hence some very suggestive entries in churchwardens' books for such interesting curative arts as "salting the fleas."

The Puritan movement received its highest expression in the allegorical poem of the "Fairy Queen." The Red Cross Knight is the Church militant, and when Arthur gives him the diamond-box, holding the water of life,

> ——"The Red-cross Knight him gave
> A book, wherein his Saviour's testament
> Was writ with golden letters, rich and brave,
> A work of wondrous grace, and able souls to save."

Una is Elizabeth symbolised, and the scarlet-clad Duessa is Catholicism, as typified in Mary Queen of Scots. Puritanism, to his poetic mind, was simply the ideal religion. invested with the grace of chivalry, and informed with a tender Platonism. It is not for us to write the history of this great movement. It welled up, like a fine spring, and ran its rippling way in many directions, not always as pure as its source, or to be recognised as coming from its original impulse. Earnest and intense religion could hardly be bright and cheerful when gaiety of heart was associated with fine clothing and loose manners. Hence it became poor in dress, plain in ceremony, austere in temper, and Calvinistic in theology. It was a revolt against luxury and a certain intellectual effeminacy—preaching duty against pleasure, and the attractions of a life beyond the grave to compensate men for what they were required to surrender in sublunary things. It branched out in many forms. With the intellectual few it was purely philosophic. With the many it ran into Presbyterianism, Congregationalism, and other non-conforming varieties. Meetings were held in private houses. Wealthy persons sheltered its notable leaders, and endowed chapels and charities. The growing middle classes were charmed by it. It was healthy, vigorous, and pronounced. The Protestantism of Elizabeth was at best a compromise. The Puritans wanted a discernible change, an earnest ritual, powerful preaching, a New Testament Church. They were ready to suffer for their faith, and when James succeeded Elizabeth, they were haled to prison with painful care. Bishops grew bold and judges were severe.

Closely connected with religion was the new Poor Law. Settlement dates back, as Professor Stubbs shows, to the Statute of Labourers, and the Acts by which it was confirmed and amended. Henry VIII. compelled the respective parishes to keep their own poor. Edward VI. had beggars branded with the letter **V**, and Elizabeth was severe as to "stalwart and valiant" mendicants, who flooded the country. No doubt the dissolution of the religious houses had made the question of pauperism more pressing. If the monks gave too little to the poor, still it was possible to say, as Selden did, that "now where XX. pound was yearly given to the poore, in more than c. places in Ingeland is not one meale's meate given." Trade guilds had assisted in providing for their own poor. Compulsory alms were ordered by Elizabeth, and a three years' residence was made a settlement. But her two most notable reforms were the Act of 1575 and the final Act of 1601. The first ordered corporate towns to deliver wool, flax, and iron, to the overseers of the poor, "so that, when poore and needy, persons, willing to work, may be set on work." The second transformed the annual poor collection of the parish church into a fixed burden to be levied on the parish itself, and the churchwardens, who had hitherto had the care of the poor, were to be assisted by overseers, nominated annually in Easter week, with power to elect a special body for large parishes. Support was to be provided for the disabled poor, and work for the rest. Entries of flax in the parish books are, in many instances, the only records of this change; the Poor-House, or Workhouse, being of later date. Apparently, there are only two allusions in Shakespeare to such things. The "working-house of thought," in the chorus to the fifth act of *Henry V.* is doubtful, because the play is usually dated before 1601. But the second is clear, and it has a touch of satire in it. *Pericles* was written after the "43rd of Elizabeth" that Carlyle so studiously reviles. The second fisherman drawing up his net in Act ii. scene 1, says, "Help, master, help! here's a fish hangs in the net like a poor man's right in the law; 'twill hardly come out."

The state of education was almost as unsettled as that of religion. The Universities of Cambridge and Oxford were thronged with poor scholars, and eminent professors taught in the schools and colleges. But the Reformation had made sad havoc with their buildings and libraries, and the spirit of amusement had affected their students. The knowledge of Greek had sensibly declined, but Latin was still cultivated with considerable success. Logic, rhetoric, mathematics, with a smattering of astronomy and physics, were also taught. The new learning gave Cambridge a special position, and Bodley's munificence had endowed Oxford with a splendid library. The study of law was diligently carried on in the Temple and the London Inns of Court, even by men who had no thought of competing for honours in Westminster Hall.

The public schools were fairly thriving, in some

instances. St. Paul's, in London, had educated Camden, and was soon to reckon among its scholars the poet Milton. Camden had been head-master at Westminster school, and it had educated Hakluyt, Ben Jonson, Giles Fletcher the poet, George Herbert, and William Heminge, a fellow actor with Shakespeare. Nicholas Udel, noted as a man of many stripes, was head-master of Eton during a part of Shakespeare's life. The Charterhouse, Harrow, and Rugby, were yet to be. Numerous grammar-schools were in existence, but they were confined to the old towns, and most of them had but slight endowments. Schools at Bedford, Rochdale, and Keswick, had been recently established. The traitorous corruption of the youths of the realm "by erecting grammar-schools," as Jack Cade has it, in *Henry VI.*, was not very extensive, for the amount of learning taught was limited to the classics and arithmetic. Malvolio, in *Twelfth Night*, is described as yellow-stockinged and cross-gartered, "like a pedant that keeps a school i' the church." Shakespeare constantly ridicules the masters of the time. Sir Hugh Evans, who hears William his "accidence," in the *Merry Wives of Windsor*, is a schoolmaster. Holofernes, in *Love's Labour's Lost*, is another, powdering his talk with Latin words, and drawing from Moth the cutting sarcasm that he and Sir Nathaniel, the curate (Sir being the title of a Master of Arts), had been "at a great feast of languages and stolen the scraps." Pinch, in the *Comedy of Errors*, is a less favourable specimen. He had the reputation of a conjurer, and his looks were true to the cast.

H

> "A hungry lean-faced villain,
> A mere anatomy, a mountebank,
> A threadbare juggler, and a fortune-teller,
> A needy, hollow-eyed, sharp-looking wretch."

To talk Latin and to make verses were considered necessary accomplishments. Shakespeare's own references to Horace, Cæsar, and Priscian, show that his "little Latin and less Greek" must not be too narrowly interpreted. The number of scholars of the Universities fit for schoolmasters was small. "Whereas they make one scholler they marre ten," averred Peacham, who describes one country specimen as whipping his boys on a cold morning "for no other purpose than to get himself a heate." The treatment of children generally was very severe in the Shakespearean period.

Noblemen's children were generally educated in private. It was customary to board them out at the house of a friend. The inferior gentry sent their sons and daughters to be taught manners and receive training in the houses of their once feudal superiors. They received a little learning, and attended the lord and lady at court. The love for "the squire of low degree," on the part of the young daughter of such a nobleman, was the theme of many old ballads. Young men, under such conditions, could not study very hard. They read a little Latin, listened to discourses, played on the lute or virginals (music being greatly cultivated by all classes), and learned to hunt and hawk in the park, to tilt and tourney in the castle-yard. "It was thought enough for a nobleman's sons," said a not unfriendly observer, "to wind their horn, carry their hawk fair, and leave study and learning to mean people."

Travel in Germany, France, and Italy, was regarded as the completion of education. Music, mathematics, fencing, fortification, and novel-reading, were all to be studied under eminent masters or wits in the foreign cities. The polished manners, the fantastic attire, the fastidious appetite, were all well-known marks of the fine gentleman who had studied in Rome, Padua, or Venice. Ascham and others lamented these enchantments, and lifted their voices aganst them. They said they were turning men's thoughts from the Bible to Boccaccio, from St. Paul to Petrarch. The virtues of the old Italians had given place to wantonness. "Italie now," protested Ascham, "is not that Italie that it was wont to be: and therefore not so fit a place, as some do count it, for young men to fetch either wisdom or honesty from thence." It was nevertheless the centre of the polite learning of the age. The printing presses of Venice were constantly publishing some novelty in poetry, politics, or romance. The influence of the second of these pursuits, as books like Harrington's "Oceana" show, was not less marked than those of the first and last. Fair Rosalind is twitting Jaques when she says, "Farewell, Monsieur Traveller. Look you lisp, and wear strange suits; disable all the benefits of your own country; be out of love with your nativity; and almost chide God for making you that countenance that you are, or I will scarce think you have swam in a gondola."

The common people were densely ignorant. They had to pick up their mother tongue as best they could. The first English Grammar was not published until 1586. It is evident that much schooling was impossible, for the necessary books did not exist. The horn-book for teaching the alphabet would almost exhaust the resources of any common day-schools that might exist in the towns and villages. Little, if any, English was taught even in the lower classes of the grammar-schools, and this fact accounts for the wonderful varieties in spelling proper names common to the period. When there is a scarcity of writing and printing, language is unsettled and variable. The art of writing was a great accomplishment. In many of the presentments made by the juries of the time, the tell-tale cross preserves its record of their deficiencies. Upon such a people the influence of the drama was sure to be irresistible, and to lift them into a new world of enchanted life.

CHAPTER VII.

SCIENCE AND SUPERSTITION.

Unscientific Character of the Elizabethans—Bruno, Bacon, and the Copernican System—Gilbert, Harvey, and Medical Science—Whims of the Learned—Popular Medicine—Royal Cures—Precious Stones as Charms—Astrology—Dr. Dee—Alchemy—The Belief in Witchcraft—Laws against it—Shakespearean Witches—Spirits—Wonders and Omens—Telling Ghost Stories—Plants, Animals, and Days—Impossible for Shakespeare to escape such Influences.

THE English of the Elizabethan age were an eminently unscientific people. They were hardly emancipated from the more primitive notions as to the constitution of the earth, the solar system, and the heavenly bodies. The acquisitions of real knowledge were mixed up with a good deal of Platonic mysticism, and the dabblers were prone to conceal their arts under the guise of magic and intercourse with invisible beings. The common people had nothing but their fancies to help them, and they allowed them the license of unbridled freedom. Forests, moors, and fens, the air, the clouds, and the waters, were all full of a life different from ours, sometimes in sympathy, frequently hostile, and not seldom revealing to men and women their future fate, their past actions, or their present dangers. Hard, coarse, gay, and mirthful, only now and then touched by the poetry of a mind like Shakespeare's into obstinate questioning of invisible things, the people were yet as timid in the darkness as children, and as full of superstitions as an egg is of meat.

The Universities did little or nothing to instruct in natural philosophy, either for the want of the men to teach, or the means to pay them. During his visit to Oxford, in 1583, Giordano Bruno, the versatile and enterprising Italian, had indeed endeavoured to teach something of the Copernican system of astronomy. It was said that he easily refuted the learned doctors who maintained that the sun revolved round the earth; but that idea continued to be generally accepted for many years afterwards. Even our great scientific luminary, Lord Bacon, was unable to accept the teaching of Copernicus, and referred to its author as "a man who thinks nothing of introducing fictions of any kind into nature, provided his calculations turn out well." His "Advancement of Learning" appeared in 1605. In spite of the place he holds in our scientific literature, Lord Bacon was himself, in many important respects, a bungler. He despised mathematics, and yet they were to prove a mighty instrument in Newton's hands. He doubted the advantage of astronomical instruments, about the time that Galileo was reading the heavens by the aid of the telescope, and discovering new wonders in its depths. The magnetic investigations of William Gilbert, most of which remain unquestioned at the present day, were spoken of by Lord Bacon with contempt. In fact, there is much truth in Harvey's saying that "the Lord Chancellor wrote on science like a Lord Chancellor."

Gilbert's discoveries in terrestrial magnetism were published in the year 1600, and it was in this very year that Harvey commenced his course of lectures at Oxford, in which he announced his views as to the circulation of the blood, though the formal publication of them did not take place until later. It seems almost impossible for a modern mind to realise what was the condition of medical science in which there were no true ideas of circulation; but the medical men of the Elizabethan and Jacobean period were of a very indifferent character. They were blind leaders of the blind. The man of science was always more or less of an alchemist, and the students of medicine were usually extensive dealers in charms and philtres. If a man wanted bleeding he went to a barber-surgeon, and when he required medicines he consulted an apothecary. The shop of the latter is well described by Shakespeare:—

> "And in his needy shop a tortoise hung,
> An alligator stuffed, and other skins
> Of ill-shaped fishes; and about his shelves
> A beggarly account of empty boxes,
> Green earthen pots, bladders, and musty seeds,
> Remnants of pack-thread and old cakes of roses
> Were thinly scattered to make up a show."

The apothecary himself was a man "in tattered weeds, with overwhelming brows," as ready to sell love-philtres to a maiden as narcotics to a friar, and not of much use for anything else, unless it were to help a desperate man to get rid of an enemy. Poisons, in fact, were much better understood than remedies.

The whims even the learned allowed themselves cannot now be described without a smile. Lord Bacon compiled a list of things tending to promote longevity that must strike Mr. Thoms with astonishment. Every morning the patient was to inhale the fume of lign-aloes, rosemary, and bay-leaves dried, "but once a week to add a little tobacco, without otherwise taking it in a pipe." For supper he was to drink of wine in which "gold had been quenched," and to eat bread dipped in spiced wine. In the morning he was to anoint the body with oil of almonds and salt and saffron. Once a month he was to bathe the feet in water of marjoram, fennel, and sage. Exercise was to be obtained in the "agitation of beer by ropes or in wheelbarrows," and that diet was pronounced best "which makes lean and then renews." The great people were content with nothing less than extravagant remedies. Salt or chloride of gold was taken by noble ladies, dissolved pearls were supposed to have mystic virtues, and even coral was a fashionable medicine. Queen Elizabeth had a great aversion to taking physic, and she showed her good sense in avoiding powdered diamonds and the inert salts of gold.

Common folk had to submit to more desperate remedies. They were advised by Dr. Andrew Boorde, from whom we derive the title of "Merry Andrew," to wipe their faces daily with a scarlet cloth, and wash them only once a week. Pills made of the skull of a man that had been hanged, a draught of spring water from the skull of a murdered man the powder of a mummy, the oil of scorpions, the blood of dragons, and the different entrails of wild animals, were all recommended for special diseases. Salves, conserves, cataplasms, ptisans, and electuaries, were made of all kinds of herbs, and freely used and believed in, though most of them must have been entirely inefficacious. The "nonsense-confused compounds," which Burton ridiculed half a century later were in great demand, however, and the amount of general physic-taking was marvellous. Complexion-washes for ladies and fops, love-philtres for the melancholy, and anodynes for the aged, were commonly dispensed in every apothecary's establishment.

Tumours were supposed to be curable by stroking them with the hand of a dead man. Chips of a hangman's tree were a great remedy for the ague, worn as amulets. To cure a child of rickets, it was passed, head downwards, through a young tree split open for the purpose, and then tied up. As the tree healed the child recovered. The king's evil, a scrofulous affection, was supposed to be cured by the royal touch. There is a description of the process in *Macbeth*:—

> *Doctor.* Ay, Sir, there are a crew of wretched souls
> That stay his cure: their malady convinces
> The great assay of art; but, at his touch—
> Such sanctity hath heaven given his hand—
> They presently amend.
> *Macduff.* What's the disease he means?

Malcolm. 'Tis called the evil,
A most miraculous work in this good king;
Which often since my here-remain in England
I have seen him do. How he solicits heaven,
Himself knows best: but strangely-visited people,
All swoln and ulcerous, pitiful to the eye,
The mere despair of surgery, he cures,
Hanging a golden stamp about their necks,
Put on with holy prayers: and 'tis spoken,
To the succeeding royalty he leaves
The healing benediction.

The Royal Society had not yet been founded, and the only learned association was the Society of Antiquaries, formed by Archbishop Parker in 1572, meeting weekly in the apartments of Sir William Detluke, in the Herald's Office, and dissolved by James I., "from some jealousy," remarks Hallam, about the year 1604. Consequently, there were no influences at work to stem the popular superstitions, and individuals who profited by them were not likely to turn reformers. The trade in charms was, however, more than half sanctioned by the learned. In his Natural History, Lord Bacon lays it down as credible that precious stones "may work by consent upon the spirits of men to comfort and exhilarate them. Those that are best for that effect are the diamond, the emerald, the hyacinth, Oriental, and the gold stone, which is the yellow topaz. As for their particular properties, there is no credit to be given to them. But it is manifest that light, above all things, excelleth in comforting the spirits of men; and it is very probable that light varied doth the same effect, with more novelty, and this is one of the causes why precious stones comfort." Bracelets of coral are recommended to cool the body, because coral loseth colour through "distemper of heat;" and other varieties for similar purposes. The learned Chancellor was thus not many degrees from the ladies and gentlemen who imagined that every precious stone had some mystic virtue, communicable to the wearer. The sapphire was believed to impart courage, the coral to preserve from enchantment, the topaz to cure madness, and the hyacinth to protect from lightning. As for the carbuncle, with its brilliant unborrowed light, it is referred to many times by Shakespeare, but perhaps in the happiest form in *Henry VIII.*, where the Princess Elizabeth is spoken of as

> "A gem
> To lighten all this isle."

Texts of Scripture, mystic letters, cabalistic rings, and other devices, were commonly worn even by the most intelligent.

Traces of a belief in astrology are to be found in Bacon, who always reflects the stronger popular impression. Queen Elizabeth was a firm believer in the science. The date of her coronation was fixed by Dr. Dee, the Mortlake astrologer, as the result of a stellar consultation, made at the request of Dudley. The Queen was afterwards very friendly with the sage. She made him Chancellor of St. Paul's, and employed him in investigating the titles and conditions of her new dominions. The rolls containing his reports are still to be seen in the Cottonian Library. His treatise on the reformation of the calendar is preserved in the Ashmolean Library, Oxford. Elizabeth consulted Dr. Dee several times for her ailments, and in her final illness he predicted that she would die at Whitehall. Her death actually took place at Richmond. The popular belief was even more intense, and the astrologer was a common figure at country fairs, where he raised the devil or cast a horoscope for a fee. In Shakespeare's tragedy of *King Lear* the old and the new faith are cleverly placed in conjunction in the characters of Gloucester, and Edmund his bastard son. Gloucester says, "These late eclipses in the sun and moon portend no good to us: though the wisdom of nature can reason it thus and thus, yet nature finds itself scourged by the sequent effects. Love cools, friendship falls off, brothers divide: in cities, mutinies; in countries, discord; in palaces, treason; and the bond cracked between son and father." Edmund laughs at the whole thing as "the excellent foppery of the world." "Sick in fortune—often the surfeit of our own behaviour—we make guilty of our disasters, the sun, the moon, and the stars: as if we were villains by necessity; fools by heavenly compulsion; knaves, thieves, and treachers, by spherical predominance; drunkards, liars, and adulterers, by an enforced obedience of planetary influence; and all that we are evil in, by a divine thrusting on."

Dr. Dee was equally famous as an alchemist. He had evidently studied the writings of Paracelsus, and after he made the acquaintance of Edward Kelly, an apothecary, who was said to have received the philosopher's stone from Germany, he plunged into mysticism, professing to hold converse with spirits, and writing accounts of his visions for the benefit of posterity. The common people broke into his house during his absence, and destroyed his instruments and manuscripts. He himself denied that he had anything to do with evil spirits, but he claimed intercourse with good ones, and the power of making gold out of baser metals. His allegorical visions were of the usual mystic character. He was an extremely able man, however, and his chemical studies were valuable. Ben Jonson's play of *The Alchemist* shows that he had studied the matter thoroughly, and was impressed with some of its follies. It is not necessary to say more here than to acknowledge that both astrology and alchemy have been of great service to mankind. Without the first we should have been deprived of much valuable astronomical forecasting, and without the second, chemistry and metallurgy would not have been so vigorously developed.

A belief in witchcraft was logically connected with the condition of science and the common superstitions. Eminent divines were as satisfied on the point as they were about the character of the Bible or the nature of the Deity. Although he exposed the vulgar errors of the period, Sir Thomas Browne was a devout believer in witches, and he declared that persons who denied their existence were infidels and atheists. The religious and dramatic literature of the time is saturated with this belief in witchcraft. Bacon regarded it as declination from true religion; and this was the ecclesiastical view. With the common people witchcraft was a mixture of good and evil, but the evil predominated. An old woman who gathered herbs, or had medical knowledge, or was a bit of a charlatan, was sure to be suspected and consulted, or shunned accordingly. Epilepsy, cross-eyes, abortions, lunacy, and diseases that physicians could not master, were all put down to witchcraft. The evil woman haunted the darkness, made compacts with the devil, directed the tempest, doomed with her curses, and destroyed by her incantations.

When Elizabeth acceded to the crown there was no law against sorcery and witchcraft. It had been repealed by Edward VI. But witches were found to have increased so terribly that she renewed it, and Bishop Jewell, in preaching before the Queen, made pointed references to the need for further action. "Your grace's subjects," he said, "pine away even unto the death; their colour fadeth, their flesh rotteth, their speech is benumbed, their senses are bereft. I pray God they never practise further than upon the subject." The occupation of the witch-finder must have been a curious one. With a pin for his instrument of search, he was permitted to prick the body of a suspected woman until he found an insensible place, or to throw her into a pond to see if she could swim, or to keep her awake until she made confessions. In the half-delirium engendered by these torments many innocent persons confessed to being witches. Reginald Scott exposed the imposture of witchcraft by a book he published in 1584, and which had something to do with the inspiration of King James's fanatical production on the subject. The king firmly believed that his stormy passage from Denmark had been caused by witches, and he attributed their activity to the approaching "consummation of the world," which made "Satan to rage the more in his instruments, knowing his kingdom to be so near an end." He increased the punishment to death, on the first conviction; and it is worthy of remark that in the Parliament which passed the law the learned Coke was Attorney-General and the scientific Bacon an active representative. Some cruel persecutions followed.

Shakespeare was no doubt in strict sympathy with current belief when he drew the portrait of Joan of Arc as a witch. Mr. Lecky regards this conception as "the darkest blot upon his genius," but this is surely a rather sweeping criticism. The poet was not likely to see in a visionary maiden the enemy of England the spotless being of modern conceptions. Talbot is made to accuse her of being a witch, serving the evil one, and entering Rouen by means of her sorceries. In the fifth act of the First Part of *Henry VI.* she is made to summon fiends before her, in terms that show the author's familiarity with the literature of witchcraft.

> "Now help, ye charming spells and periapts;
> And ye choice spirits that admonish me,
> And give me signs of future accidents:
> You speedy helpers, that are substitutes
> Under the lordly monarch of the north,
> Appear, and aid me in this enterprise!"

They enter, but speak not, hanging their heads in sign of disaster. The introduction of the witches into *Macbeth* adds powerfully to the interest of that tragedy, and in the description of their incantations and appearance Shakespeare has enriched common materials with the weird grandeur of his own imagination. To the playgoers of his time the witch scenes must have been terribly impressive. How they affected later spectators Addison has described. Sitting near a woman of quality, he says that before the curtain rose she broke out into a loud soliloquy, "When will the dear witches enter?"

All the names of the spirits referred to by Shakespeare, Graymalkin, Paddock, Setebos, Belphegor, Barbazon, and others, are to be found in Reginald Scott, or other contemporary writers on witchcraft. There was a perfect legion of spirits, and their names are themselves a curiosity. Bull-beggars, urchins, imps, elves, calcars, changelings, the Incubus, Robin Goodfellow, the spoonie, the hell-wain, the puckle, Tom Timbler, boneless, and the firedrake, were constantly referred to in common conversation. A polled sheep, as Scott expresses it, "is a perilous beast, and manie times is taken for our father's soule, specially in a churchyard." The supernatural element was as strongly believed in as anything else. Fairies danced at night round the forest oak on the village green. Headless horsemen affrighted the drunken reveller who had to cross a lonely moor on his way home. The shepherd who had not seen a spirit was as rare a being as the man who has not seen the ocean is at the present day. When Hamlet, addressing his father's ghost, asks—

> "Be thou a spirit of health or goblin damned,
> Bring with thee airs from heaven or blasts from hell,
> Be thy intents wicked or charitable,
> Thou comest in such a questionable shape,
> That I will speak to thee—"

he would make no extraordinary demand upon an audience accustomed to believe in good and evil spirits walking the earth and air at night. Nor was Shakespeare's sketch of the magician, Prospero, half so wild and fantastic as it appears to the modern reader.

Superstition was so intensely a part of the life of the time, that telling stories of far-off wonders and monstrosities was one of the nightly amusements of all classes. Othello alludes to the anthropophagi—

> "And men whose heads
> Do grow beneath their shoulders."

Gonzalo, in *The Tempest*, asks the pointed question :—

> "Who would believe that there were mountaineers
> Dewlapped like bulls, whose throats had hanging at them
> Wallets of flesh? Or that there were such men
> Whose heads stood in their breasts?"

The timid were always on the watch for hints from the unseen world, for

> "Prodigies and signs,
> Abortives, presages, and tongues of heaven."

There are numerous allusions to these omens in the plays of Shakespeare. Before the assassination of Julius Cæsar it was declared

"A lioness hath whelped in the streets;
And graves have yawned and yielded up their dead:
Fierce, fiery warriors fight upon the clouds
In ranks, and squadrons, and right forms of war,
Which drizzled blood upon the capitol:
The noise of battle hurtled in the air,
Horses did neigh, and dying men did groan,
And ghosts did shriek and squeal about the streets."

Before the murder of Duncan there were similar signs and prodigies.

"Lamentings heard in the air; strange screams of death."

The signs which foreshadow the death or fall of kings are described in *Richard II.*:—

"The bay-trees in our country are all withered
And meteors fright the fixed stars of heaven;
The pale-faced moon looks bloody on the earth,
And lean-looked prophets whisper fearful change;
Rich men look sad, and ruffians dance and leap."

Sidereal and terrestrial portents accompanied the birth of Owen Glendower and Richard III. Before death, according to Troilus, "the Genius so cries, come!" The good and evil angels that attend all mortals are specially referred to in *Henry IV.*, *Macbeth*, and *Antony and Cleopatra*. The paling lights in *Richard III.* indicate the presence of spirits. The elves and fairies of popular romance are pictured and presented with inimitable skill. Who does not remember the fine description of Queen Mab, "that plats the manes of horses in the night"?

Ghost tales were told by the firelight in nearly every household. The young were thus touched by the prevailing superstitions in their most impressionable years. They looked for the incorporeal creatures of whom they had heard, and they were quick to invest any trick of moonbeam or shadow with the attributes of the supernatural. A description of one of these tale-tellings is given in the *Winter's Tale.*

> *Hermione.* What wisdom stirs amongst you? Come, sir; now
> I am for you again: pray you sit by us,
> And tell's a tale.
> *Mamillius.* Merry or sad, shall 't be?
> *Her.* As merry as you will.
> *Mam.* A sad tale 's best for winter.
> I have one of sprites and goblins.
> *Her.* Let's have that, good sir,
> Come on, sit down; come on and do your best
> To fright me with your sprites: you 're powerful at it.
> *Mam.* There was a man.
> *Ner.* Nay, come, sit down; then on.
> *Mam.* Dwelt by a churchyard.—I will tell it softly,
> Yond crickets shall not hear it.
> *Her.* Come on then,
> And give 't me in mine ear.

The entry of other characters prevents the story, or a pretty romance would have followed, perhaps, about the owl, who "was a baker's daughter," as Ophelia says, or a pathetic account of the ruddock, or robin redbreast, so beautifully referred to by Arviragus in *Cymbeline*, or of such hounds as Prospero sends to hunt Caliban, Stephano, and Trinculo.

Plants and animals were symbols of the full spirit-life of nature. The mandrake groaned when torn out of the earth, driving the unfortunate victim mad. The eye of the toad was "a precious jewel," guarding any one who possessed it from the effects of poison. The tears of a crocodile were supposed to crystallise into a gem. The interior of a capon was said to yield a precious stone called Alectorius ; the Chelidonius came from a swallow ; Geranites, from a crane ; and Draconites out of dragons and serpents. Fern-seed made invisible the man who had it in his pocket, because it was only to be seen on St. John's Eve, and at the moment the saint was born. Hence, Gadshill says in the First Part of *Henry IV.*, "We have the receipt of fern-seed, we walk invisible." Almanacks, marking lucky or unlucky days, were published by astrologers. Webster says :—

> " By the almanack, I think,
> To choose good days, and shun the critical."

Constance, in *King John*, asks why this day should be set in golden letters in the calendar—

> " But (except) on this day, let seamen fear no wreck ;
> No bargains break, that are not this day made ;
> This day, all things begun come to an ill end ;
> Yea, faith itself to hollow falsehood change."

There were other superstitions, of a more general character, some of which still survive amongst us. Constant allusions are made to them in the dramas of Shakespeare, and it would be a bootless task to inquire whether he believed in them or not. They were a common possession, and he could no more have escaped from their influence than from the atmosphere he breathed. A world of supernaturalism affected alike the pulpit and the stage, the students of science and the gossips of the village-green. Accordingly, as we read the works of the time, we seem to pass into another sphere, and to understand the play of fancy which, enriched and spiritualised, communicates such a potent charm to plays like the *Tempest* and the *Midsummer Night's Dream.*

CHAPTER VIII.

THE COURT—ELIZABETH AND JAMES I.

The Courts of Elizabeth and James true Mirrors of the Time—The Difference of *Personnel*—The Royal Palaces—The Royal Progresses—Elizabeth's Ceremonialism—Love of Dress and Ornament—Personal Appearance—Learning—Compliments—Money Matters—James I.

THE Courts of Elizabeth and James I. had one remarkable quality, whatever else they may have lacked. They reflected the highest as well as the lowest features of the time. Weary with the mental dulness of the masses of the people, the student of character found at Court a dazzling versatility. The play of wit, the cunning epigram, the graceful sonnet, the classic citations, the affected chivalry, and, later, the theological dissertations, were extremely diverting and delightful. But, in the presence of Court jealousies, of intriguants trying to compass each other's fall, and of constant scandals, gilded vice, and, under James, open and unrebuked drunkenness, he might perhaps admit the simple virtues of plainer minds, the worth of the unlettered herd.

There was a marked difference in the *personnel* of the two courts. The Queen liked wits who played with words, embellished conversation with choice fancies, and who carefully avoided all serious problems, either of life or of state policy. The King encouraged theological controversy, for which he flattered himself he had a gift, and took an equal delight in the chatter of servants about cockfights and royal sports. The first liked to be flattered for her beauty; the second relished nothing so keenly as compliments about personal power. Lords and ladies, sturdy soldiers and bold voyagers, hung about Elizabeth, to minister to her wants, to interpret her ambitions, and to receive her smiles. Around James were Scotch gallants, fervid ecclesiastics, timid time-servers, and gossiping doctors. The one had brave councillors to advise her—Burleigh, a solid, sagacious, thorough Englishman, whose advice, according to Mr. Froude, she never rejected without going wrong; and Sir Nicholas Bacon, her Lord Keeper of the Privy Seal, whose ample form and gouty limbs induced her to say to him once, in ordering him not to rise in her presence, "My lord, we make use of you, not for your bad legs, but your good head." The other was changeable yet self-confident, leaning upon no one, preferring minions to ministers, and doing nothing to make statesmen out of the weak favourites about him. The last of the Tudors was always attended by her fifty gentlemen-pensioners, with their gilt battle-axes, as a body-guard—a contingent formed of the flower of the nobility, none of its poor privates having a less income than four thousand a year. The first of the Stuarts allowed this splendid corps to lose its lustre, preferring to sell peerages that he might make money for his own use, and to create the order of baronets that he might furnish soldiers for Ireland. Indeed, all that was good about the Court of James may be fairly described as a continuation, and nearly all that seems new presents itself to us as caricature.

When in London, Elizabeth and James lodged at Whitehall Palace. Henry VIII. had built St. James's Palace, after a design said to have been furnished by Holbein, but his daughter does not seem to have cared for the place, or even for Whitehall, which had been built by one of the wealthy Archbishops of York, and wrung from Wolsey by his sovereign. There was also the palace of Mary-le-Bonne, now Regent's Park, where the Czar's embassy had lived and hunted in 1600. There were other palaces Elizabeth much preferred. At Greenwich she had witnessed many a tilt and tourney. At Hampton Court she gave audiences to foreign ambassadors, in a room hung with splendid tapestries and shining with gold and silver. In its great hall Shakespeare and Burbage played to her and her successor, and in its squares the courtiers pitched their tents during the occasional pressure of guests and foreigners. At Windsor she revelled in a magnificence which wrung from Hentzner the German many passages of eloquent description. Here, moored in the river, she kept her royal barge with its two fine cabins and its splendid ornamentation. A very little touch of exaggeration gave to Shakespeare his description of Cleopatra:—

> "The barge she sat on, like a burnished throne,
> Burned in the water: the poop was beaten gold,
> Purple the sails, and so perfumed that
> The winds were love-sick with them."

RICHMOND PALACE.

The palace at Richmond, in Surrey, where she constantly lived and ultimately died, was an especially favourite residence. It was a collection of rectangular towers and embayed windows, and situated in the town of Richmond. A ruined gateway is the only portion now remaining. It was her great delight to climb the hill and walk in the park, discoursing to great men or personal favourites. Nonsuch Palace, near Ewell, in Surrey, another favourite residence of hers, was an architectural curiosity. It had two courts. The lower storey was of stone and the upper one of wood, adorned with statues, pictures, and devices made of rye-bread dough, with lofty towers at the eastern and western angles, balustraded, and lit with lanterns at the top. There was also a palace at Chelsea; and Elizabeth had other houses, as The Lodge at Islington, The Grove at Newington, and The Dairy at Barnelms. She moved about freely from palace to palace, as the whim seized her. A hint of the plague sent her into the country, and a whisper of urgent business brought her back again to town. James I. moved between London and Edinburgh, for the most part, hunting in Sherwood and Gaultre Forest by the way. On one occasion the common people ran so much to see him, on his return from hunting, that, so the French ambassador reported, "he cursed every one he met, and swore that if they did not let him follow the chase at his pleasure he would leave England." Elizabeth, with her customary tact, would have made a gracious speech on such an occasion, which would have contained some clever reference to English sport.

The Royal progresses of the time were costly, imposing, and yet popular events. The people always like to see a monarch unbend, and there was real delight in the gay processions from place to place and mansion to mansion. The richly-caparisoned horses, the brilliant costumes, the blare of trumpet and throb of drum, the ringing of church bells, the green arches by the way, and the masks, revels, and plays, at night, were all parts of a pageantry the like of which had never before been seen. Elizabeth made twenty-five state progresses during her reign, hunting as she went, and feasting, with her Court, at the expense of nobles who could sometimes ill afford to entertain her. The receptions at Elvetham and Kenilworth, the ceremonies of the visit to Cambridge, Norwich, and Oxford, would require many pages to describe with anything like conscientious detail. It is, perhaps, of more interest we should know that she behaved with the utmost courtesy to all about her, permitting the common people to have free access to her, taking and instantly reading their petitions, and assuring them of her interest in their affairs. It was by such means as these that she won her title of "Good Queen Bess." Her condescension was charming, while the defects of her personal character and public policy were invisible. James continued the progresses in a clumsy and haughty manner. The form and tints of the rose remained, but its perfume had departed.

Elizabeth liked to have tall and active men about her. Her chamberlains, carvers, ushers, cup-bearers,

A ROYAL PROGRESS—QUEEN ELIZABETH'S VISIT TO HUNSDON HOUSE, 1571. (From a painting ascribed to Mark Gerard, and engraved in Vertue's "Historical Prints.")

grooms, and trumpeters were all shapely, athletic fellows, distinguished by their good looks, and liable, it is said, to lose their place if they lost a front tooth. Stately ceremonial was her especial pride. Her secretaries knelt down before her to deliver a letter, kissed it, and then placed it in her hands, remaining motionless until her commands were received. She went to prayers in procession, with all her royal paraphernalia before her. Her meal tables were laid with elaborate forms. An usher with a white wand entered the hall, attended by a servant bearing the cloth. Kneeling thrice in succession, the cloth was spread, and then, kneeling again, they retired. The usher came in with each servant bearing the various articles for the table—a salt-cellar, a plate, the bread, a cup—kneeling thrice before and once after placing each thing on the cloth. Two ladies then followed, kneeling like the others, in spite of their gorgeous silk dresses. The first bore the tasting-knife, the second rubbed the plate with bread and salt. The yeomen of the guard succeeded, in their scarlet suits, with a golden rose on their backs, bringing in the dishes and viands. Received with stately courtesy by the usher, the lady-taster gave them each a portion of their food to eat, trumpets and kettle-drums sounding the while. When the music ceased, her eight maids of honour appeared—"gentle Howard, tall Dacres, modest Baynam, wise Arundell, beautiful Dormer, merry Mancell, learned Coke, and pious Bridges"—and carried off a portion of the food to the Queen's private chamber. When she dined in public she was waited upon by noblemen. Leicester's stately living and display in the Netherlands roused her jealousy, and, when the news reached her, she exclaimed that she would "let the upstart know how easily the hand which had exalted him could lay him in the dust."

Her love of jewellery and personal magnificence was extreme. As her personal charms decayed she increased the brilliancy of her adornments. The gifts she exacted from her favourites on New Year's Day would have made an interesting collection. Gold ornaments and watches, jewels, fans, fantastic love-tokens, rich robes, even embroidered body-linen, and gold crowns from ecclesiastics, were parts of the customary gifts of courtiers and favour-seekers. Her side-saddle of black velvet, embroidered with pearls and gold, with harness of silk and gold, is mentioned amongst the Domestic State Papers of her reign as costing £266 13s. 4d. of the money of the time. Hentzner describes her books at Whitehall as being bound in red velvet, with clasps of gold and silver, "and pearls and precious stones set in their bindings." Lady Capulet says:—

> "That book in many eyes doth share the glory
> That in gold clasps locks in the golden story."

Harrington says of Vaughan and his sophism, by which he attributed her miraculous healing-power to some precious stone in her possession, that if she had known that he "ascribed more virtue to her jewels, though she loved them well, than to her person she had never made him Bishop of Chester." Her love of fine dresses was quite a passion. Marvellous costumes, covered with eyes and ears, to represent omniscience, with birds and animals, flowers and fruits, and various allegorical devices, were constantly worn by her, and exhibited in triumph to her ambassadors. She might preach simplicity of costume to others, but she never practised it herself.

Her personal appearance had once been distinguished, if not handsome. Slight in build and stature, with yellow hair, a high forehead, dark and lively eyes, but weak of sight (as was also the case with Mary Queen of Scots), she had a finely-chiselled nose, a firmly-set mouth, a sharp chin, and a pale, clear complexion. She prided herself greatly on the beauty of her hands and fingers. Foreign observers noticed, however, that her teeth were black, and they attributed the fact to her large consumption of sugar, of which she was inordinately fond, in the shape of Portingals, or Portuguese confectionery. Her carriage was dignified and majestic. Amongst her papers is the draft of an undated proclamation, which was never issued, prohibiting "payntors, pryntors, and gravors" from drawing and issuing her picture until "some person mete therefor shall make a natural representation of Her Majesty's person, favour, or grace," as a pattern for others to copy. The reference is possibly to caricatures, but there is evidence that some portraits were destroyed.

Of her learned acquirements there is ample evidence. She could speak French, though with a drawling accent, perhaps peculiar to the time, as well as Italian, Latin, and Greek. She read Cicero, Livy, Sophocles, St. Cyprian, Socrates, Seneca, and Melancthon. She composed sonnets, epigrams, and spirit-stirring speeches. Harrison remarks that a stranger suddenly entering her Court would "imagine himself to come into some public school of the Universities." Despite her culture and insinuating speech, sweet and gentle as the air of morning, as one said who knew her well, she used terrible oaths, round and full; she stamped her feet, she thrust about her with a sword, she spat upon her attendants, and behaved, as the French said, like "a lioness." "With her for a queen, were I a monarch," said Pope Sixtus V., "we should conquer and rule the world." But she had her moods of tenderness. Over Mary's piteous letter, after the death-fiat had gone forth, she shed real tears, and many a touching note from her pen reached bereaved subjects. Delight in singing-birds, pet animals, and little children, was quite consistent with her haughty bearing to disgraced favourites and threatening enemies. Music, especially her virginals, enabled her, she said, "to shun melancholy."

Compliments were natural to the time, and to her position. She especially enjoyed being called the "Virgin Queen," and nothing was more to her taste than Shakespeare's reference to her as "the fair vestal throned by the West," who resisted the shafts of Cupid, and went on her way, "in maiden meditation, fancy free." It was but a free rendering of her own reply to her people, in 1559, when they wished her to marry.

"As for mee, it shall be sufficient that a marble stone shall declare that a Queene, having lived and reigned so many yeeres, died a virgin." Spenser refers to her in his "Fairy Queen" under the characters of Una, Gloriana, Belphœbe, and Mercillæ. In "Colin Clout" she is the Shepherdess, Cynthia, the Lady of the Sea, of whom he says—

> "But if I her like ought on earth might read,
> I would her liken to a crown of lillies
> Upon a virgin bride's adorned head,
> With Roses dight, and goolds and daffodillies,
> Or like the circlet of a Turtle true,
> In which all colours of the rainbow be;
> Or like fair Phœbe's girland shining new,
> In which all pure perfection one may see.
> But vain it is to think by paragone
> Of earthly things, to judge of things divine:
> Her power, her mercy, her wisdome, none
> Can deeme, but who the Godhead can define."

The epitaph hung up in many churches at her death was just as bold in its ending—

> "She is—she was—what can there more be said?
> On earth the first, in heaven the second maid."

The sickliness of the classic compliments paid to her, comparing her to Diana, to Venus, to Orpheus, even after Time's effacing fingers had touched her beauty, must have impressed her now and then with their falsity. Whilst others hungered after the simple joys of pastoral and woodland life, it is impossible she can have wholly escaped from dreaming of a true and less artificial existence, amidst honesty and naturalness,

Ascham noted in her, as a pupil, the power of immediately detecting "any ill-adapted or far-fetched expression," and this discernment must often have enabled her to pierce through the adulation of her courtiers, the compliments of the phrase-makers. It would serve her well when Philip, Ivan the Terrible, and the Duke of Alençon, pressed for her hand, and Leicester, Raleigh, and Essex, fluttered about her like gorgeous butterflies.

Elizabeth's parsimony is constantly dwelt upon by the historians. No doubt it was marked. The country was poor, and she was unwilling to tax it. There were wealthy nobles, and she took care to make them contribute to the services of the realm; but she raised money in ways that remind us of the customs of Russia and Turkey. The Privy Council loans were forced contributions, for which paper promises were given, rarely redeemed in a hurry. Any one who was known to have amassed a sum of ready money might receive, without any notice, an order from the nearest magistrate, signed with the Privy Seal, saying that the Queen would become his debtor to a given amount. If Elizabeth rewarded her favourites, she had few honours and little largesse for her devoted Ministers, who sometimes impoverished themselves in her service. The giving and taking of bribes was one of the worst features of the time. Archbishops and minor folk did not hesitate to send money with their requests, and ministers and judges took it with unblushing eagerness, frequently without rendering the slightest equivalent. Burleigh sold Church preferments, and Lord Bacon had accepted presents from suitors; but they might have pleaded a royal example, possibly a poor salary, if not a pure intent. The casuistry of such matters does not concern us here. Yet, in the face of Elizabeth's treacheries and dissimulation, we must admit her greatness, her English heart, her single-minded desire for the glory of the realm she ruled. Few lives, as Mr. Froude is compelled to acknowledge, will "bear so close a scrutiny, and yield less shame and dismay."

It is hardly necessary to say much of King James. His struggle with Protestantism and Parliament, and his attachment to the giddy adventurer Villiers, were the main features of his rule. In personal appearance he was awkward and ungainly. His weak legs compelled him to loll about on other men's shoulders. Large and prominent eyes gave him a curious, uncanny appearance. The slobbering way in which he talked, owing to his tongue being too long for his mouth, and the quantity he drank, made him a fit theme for the satire of his subjects. His Scotch accent, his worn garments, his extravagant expenditure upon low forms of amusement, and his slovenliness and *abandon*, were not calculated to impress his courtiers or to please his people. If he swam witches to show his aversion to superstition in others, he touched for the king's evil to display his own miraculous divinity. Yet was he wise and witty, sententious and shrewd, with all the weakness of a despot, and few of the virtues that sometimes brighten an imperious disposition. He wanted the fibre, the tact, the chivalrous disposition of his predecessor. Under his connivance, if not sanction, the Court ceased to veil its debaucheries, or to regard drunkenness as anything more serious than a royal weakness.

CHAPTER IX.

SHAKESPEARE'S LONDON.

The City a Wonder—Its External Appearance—The River and its Mansions — Alsatia — Bankside and its Associations — London Bridge—A Stroll with Jonson and Shakespeare—Fish Hill—East Chepe—London Stone—The Exchange—Cheapside—The Mermaid Tavern — St. Paul's — Fleet Street — General Impressions.

THE London of the period was not so gay as Paris, nor so bustling and prosperous as Antwerp, nor so full of splendour and intellectual life as Venice. Yet to the Englishman of the day it was an everlasting wonder. Its towers and palaces, its episcopal residences and gentlemen's inns, the beauty of the Thames, the bustle of its commerce, the number of its foreigners, the wealth of its Companies, and the bravery of its pageants, invested it with more poetry than can be claimed for it at the present time, unless Wealth be our deity, Hurry our companion, and Progress our muse. The rich were leaving their pleasant country mansions to plunge into its delights. At the law terms there was a regular influx of visitors, who seemed to think more of taking tobacco than of winning a law-suit. Ambitious courtiers, hopeful ecclesiastics, pushing merchants, and poetic dreamers, were all caught by the fascinations of London. Site, antiquity, life, and, above all, abundance of the good things that make up half its charms, in the shape of early delicacies, costly meats, and choice wines, combined to make it a miraculous city in the eyes of the Elizabethan. Drayton, who does not soar very high, and who recognises the material comforts we have just referred to, endeavoured to express the prevailing feeling when he broke out :—

> "O more than mortal man that did this town begin,
> Whose knowledge found the plot so fit to set it in,
> As in the fittest place by man that could be thought,
> To which by sea or land provisions could be brought.
> And such a road for ships scarce all the world commands
> As is the goodly Thames, near where Brute's city stands."

The external appearance of the city was certainly picturesque. Old grey walls threw round it the arm of military protection. Their gates were conspicuous objects, and the white uniforms of the train-bands on guard, with their red crosses on the back, fully represented the valour which wraps itself in the British flag and dies in its defence. To the north were the various fields whose names survive, diversified by an occasional house, and Dutch-looking windmills creaking in the breeze. Finsbury was a fenny tract, where the City archers practised ; Spitalfields, an open grassy place, with grounds for artillery exercise and a market cross ; and Smithfield, or Smoothfield, was an unenclosed plain, where tournaments were held, horses were sold, and martyrs had been burnt. To the east was the Tower of London, black with age, armed with cannon and culverin, and representing the munificence which entertained royalty as well as the power which

THE TOWER OF LONDON IN SHAKESPEARE'S TIME

punished traitors. Beyond it was Wapping, the Port of London, with its narrow streets, its rope-walks, and biscuit shops. Black-fronted taverns, with low doorways and leaden-framed windows, their rooms reeking with smoke, and noisy with the chatter of ear-ringed sailors, were to be found in nearly every street. Here the merchant adventurer came to hire his seamen, and here the pamphleteer or the ballad-maker could any night gather materials for many a long-winded yarn about Drake and the Spanish Main, negroes, pearls, and palm-groves.

To the west the scene was broken with hamlets, trees, and country roads. Marylebone and Hyde Park were a royal hunting-ground, with a manor-house, where the Earls of Oxford lived in later times. Piccadilly was "the road to Reading," with foxgloves growing in its ditches, gathered by the simple dealers to make anodynes for the weary-hearted. Chelsea was a village; Pimlico a country hamlet, where pudding-pies were eaten by strolling Londoners on a Sunday. Westminster was a city standing by itself, with its Royal Palace, its Great Hall for banquets and the trial of traitors, its sanctuary, its beautiful Abbey, and its famous Almonry. King Street was full of shops, yet so ill-kept was its roadway that when Sovereigns went to open Parliament bundles of faggots had to be thrown into its holes that the carriages might run safely. In this street the poet Spenser lived when in town, and here he came to die after he had been hunted from Ireland. St. James's Park was walled with red brick, and contained the palace Henry VIII. had built for Anne Boleyn. Whitehall Palace was in its glory. Charing was a hamlet. The Strand, along which gay ladies drove in their "crab-shell coaches," had been recently paved, and its streams of water diverted. A few houses had made their appearance on the north side of the Strand, between the timber house and its narrow gateway, which then formed Temple Bar, the boundary between London and Westminster, and the church of St. Mary-le-Strand. The southern side was adorned with noble episcopal residences, and with handsome turreted mansions, extending to the river, rich with trees and gardens, and relieved by flashes of sparkling water.

To the south, Lambeth, with its palace and church, and Faux Hall, were conspicuous objects. Here were pretty gardens and rustic cottages. The village of Southwark, with its prison, its theatre, its palace, and its old Tabard Inn, had many charms. It was, as we shall see, the abode of Shakespeare himself.

Surrounded by thriving hamlets and villages, by splendid oaks and beeches, by quaint windmills and palatial houses, with its sky-line broken by walls, towers, and high-pitched roofs, and the fluttering of many flags, the exterior of London, with little but wood-smoke to dull the brightness of the atmosphere, presented quite a gay and charming picture.

We must not forget the River Thames. It was one of the sights of the time. Its waters were pure and bright, full of delicate salmon, and flecked by snowy swans, "white as Lemster wool." Wherries plied freely on its surface. Tall masts clustered by

OLD SOMERSET HOUSE, LONDON.

its banks. Silken-covered tiltboats, freighted with ruffed and feathered ladies and gentlemen, swept by, the watermen every now and then breaking the plash of the waves against their boats by singing out, in their bass voices, "Heave and how, rumbelow." At night the scene reminded the travelled man of Venice. All the mansions by the waterside had river-terraces and steps, and each one its own tiltboat, barge, and watermen. Down these steps, lighted by torches and lanterns, stepped dainty ladies in their coloured shoes, with masks on their faces, and gay gallants, in laced cloaks, by their side, bound for Richmond or Westminster, to mask and revel. Noisy parties of wits and Paul's men crossed to Bankside, to see *Romeo and Juliet* or *Hamlet the Dane.* Lights flashed, waves rippled, guitars were thrummed, and pathetic ballads smoothed

> "the raven down
> Of darkness, till it smiled!"

From Westminster to London Bridge was a favourite trip. There was plenty to see. The fine Strand-side houses were always pointed out—Northumberland House, York House, Durham House, Salisbury House, Savoy Palace, Somerset House, Bath's Inn, Essex House, the Temple and its gardens. Baynard's Castle, the scene of the secret interview between the Duke of York and the Earls of Salisbury and Warwick, was singled out, between Paul's Wharf and Puddle Dock. Next to the Temple, and between it and Whitefriars, was the region known as

Alsatia, described by Sir Walter Scott in his "Fortunes of Nigel." Safe from every document but the writ of the Lord Chief Justice and the Lords of the Privy Council, here in dark dwellings, with subterranean passages, narrow streets, and trap-doors that led to the Thames, dwelt all the rascaldom of the time—men who had been "horned" or outlawed (the Tothills of our time are the places where the horn was formerly *tooted*), bankrupts, coiners, thieves, cheaters at dice and cards, duellists, homicides, and foreign bravoes, ready to do any desperate deed. At night the contents of this kingdom of villainy were sprayed out over London, to the bewilderment of good-natured Dogberries, and country gentlemen making their first visit to town.

A little lower down the river, on its southern shore, is a spot which interests us intensely. Between what are now Blackfriars and Southwark Bridges is a strip of land called Bankside. Here stands the Globe Theatre—not handsome, certainly, but likely to be immortal. Here also is Paris Garden, famous for its bear-baiting, and alive on Sunday with burgesses and their wives, apprentices and their sweethearts, come to see Saccarson perform. The Bear Gardens were close by, where Stowe says, "he kept bears, bulls, and other beasts to be baited, as also mastiffs in several kennels, nourished to bait them. These bears and other beasts are there kept in plots of ground, scaffolded about for the beholders to stand safe." It was here the French Ambassador was conducted by Elizabeth's orders to see the English sports. Massinger, Beaumont, and Fletcher, lived on Bankside. Of the last Aubrey writes, "I have supped with him at his house on the Bankside; he loved a fat loin of pork of all things in the world." At the Falcon Inn, near Paris Gardens, Shakespeare and his fellow-players and writers supped many an evening after the performances at the Globe. Shakespeare himself lived "in the liberty of the Clink," and his house was somewhere in Clink Street. As he grew more prosperous, he purchased a dwelling on the opposite shore, "near the Wardrobe," but he does not seem to have occupied it. At his death it came by his will to Susannah Hall, his daughter; and it was described as "now or late in the tenure or occupacion of William Ireland."

Still further down the river was the famous London Bridge. It consisted of twenty arches; its roadway was sixty feet from the river; and the length of the bridge from end to end was 926 feet. It was one of the wonders that strangers never ceased to admire. Its many shops were occupied by pinnacres, just beginning to feel the competition with the Netherland pin-makers, and the tower at its Southwark end was adorned with three hundred heads, stuck on poles, like gigantic pins, memorials of treachery and heresy. The roar of the river through the arches was almost deafening. "The noise at London Bridge is nothing near her," says one of the characters in Beaumont and Fletcher's *Woman's Prize.* Shakespeare and Ben Jonson must have crossed the bridge many a time on their visits to the City, to "gather humours of men daily," as Aubrey quaintly expresses it.

If we take a stroll with them along the main thoroughfares, we may see some of the sights of the time. Not delaying to look at the rows of London pins in the window, we have reached the City itself. Here to the right is Fish Street Hill, up which, and "down Saint Magnus Corner," Jack Cade took his rebels, as described in the Second Part of *Henry VI.* Two inns attract our notice: the Black Bell, the former residence of Edward the Black Prince, and King's Head Tavern. Whilst we have turned to look at the fish-stalls, and priced the cod and ling in their wicker baskets, Jonson has turned into the King's Head, where he has had many a high carousal, to get a cup of canary. A little further on we come to East Chepe, white-aproned cooks crying out "Hot ribs of beef," and "Pies well baked." Is not that Sir John Falstaff, wittiest of sinners, who has just turned into the Boar's Head for refreshment, saying to Dame Quickly, who has been looking out for him, "Come, give 's some sack"? Surely, that was Bardolph's nose just visible behind the Dame's snowy cap.

Leaving the jovial knight to his sack, we proceed To our left is Cannon Street, famous for its "London Stone," standing erect on the south side of the street. Striking it with his sword, Jack Cade said, "Here, sitting on this stone, I charge and command that of the City's cost the conduit run nothing but claret wine this first year of our reign." Up Gracious (now Gracechurch) Street, with its herb market, we walk a little until we come to Fenchurch Street, an early hay-market, whilst to our left is the street of the money-lenders, coin-dealers, and pawn-takers, bearing the name of Lombard Street. At the sign of the "Grasshopper," in this street, lives Sir Thomas Gresham, the builder of the Royal Exchange. Curious foreign costumes meet the eye, reverend men of Mantua and Padua, in homely stuffs piped with red, and amongst them the Jewish gaberdine. Our route is by Cornhill, then anything but a corn-place, full of old-clothes shops and familiar Jewish physiognomies. If you have been robbed of a hat, a cloak, or a rapier, in a brawl over night, it is here you may find it hanging next morning, with a good price on it in English money.

The Exchange is a noble building. People call it the Bourse. It consists of an upper part, called the Pawn, or promenade, full of bazaars and stalls of costly goods, where ladies and gentlemen lounge in the evening, when it is brilliantly lit up: and of a lower part, piazza and quadrangle, alive with the hum of many tongues, and ejaculations about Tripoli raisins, French coats, and the price of pepper. The din of Russian, Dutch, French, and Italian, is enough to turn the brain. As it is daylight, we must look for the idlers, not in the Pawn, but at St. Paul's. To lounge in St. Paul's was euphemistically called "dining with Duke Humphrey;" to perambulate the Pawn was "to sup with Sir Thomas Gresham."

It is a relief to turn into the Poultry, and to examine the swans for the coming civic feast, all duly nicked and exhibited here, an appetising sight for the Elizabethan cockney. The London street-boy is here in full force, with his doublet and belt and his ragged woollen cap. The latter is his only weapon wherewith to beat a hostile youth. When he is a little bigger he will mount a cudgel or a knife. Fat capons that Falstaff would relish, and wild ducks fresh from Lincolnshire or the marshes of the Thames, also hang invitingly in the shops. The Trade Hall of the Grocers, or Pepperers, is hard by. To the right is the Jewerie, the abode of that persecuted but useful tribe. A little further is Bucklersbury, inhabited by druggists. The dandies, says Falstaff, "smell like Bucklersbury in simple time," the reference being more especially to rosemary and lavender, the great scents of the Elizabethans. We pass on to Cheapside, and duly note the Standard, where Lord Say was executed by the Cade rebels, the beautiful cross, recently restored, and the stone conduit, in the middle of the road, worn and grey with age, around which red-skirted and white-bodiced servant-maids are waiting to draw water. Robert Herrick, the poet, who was born here, calls it "golden Cheapside," in his "Tears to Thamasis," and the epithet is exact and true. Goldsmiths' shops, exhibiting Venice gold cups, jugs, earrings, ornaments, and plaques, are clustering together, just as the Netherland envoys saw them when they came to invoke our aid in the struggle against Philip. Persian silks, Turkey carpets, Cashmere shawls, and piles of glossy Paris thread, are visible in some of the windows, the spoils of some Spanish carack that never reached the end of her voyage. Curious eyes are upon them; a Papist in hiding glares savagely at these Catholic spoils; a jaunty Protestant thanks God, and lifts his ruffed neck a little higher in the air. The shops project on the pavement, a custom which has not yet been discontinued in some parts of London, and the tradesmen at their doors, or in front of their shops, if unglazed, press us to spend our angels and half-angels, with modulated entreaty and commendation.

Our present destination is Bread Street, however and we must examine its fair inns. Every good house is an inn, and every house has its sign, either swinging overhead, or blazoned on its second storey, or stuck daintily over its main door. Numbers are unknown. It is the "Mermaid" we are in search of; and here it is—quaint, heavily-timbered, capacious, a very presentable inn. Wealthy merchants live in the street, but it is not with them we are concerned. It is here the Mermaid Club meets, and the gentleman in the trunk-hose, with meditative air, dreamy eyes, and pointed chin, is Sir Walter Raleigh, its president, entering to make inquiries after Shakespeare and Fletcher. To-night, or possibly to-morrow night, there will be a goodly company around its square table, sitting on plain wooden chairs, and talking, as only wise and witty men do, over their malmsey and canary. We are familiar with their names—Shakespeare, Jonson, Beaumont, and Fletcher, poets all, joined by the sagacious Selden, and the whimsical Donne. To hear them, to take part in their wit-combats, to see Jonson like a Spanish galleon and gentle Willy like a light barque, Fletcher all tenderness, and Selden dry and caustic, would be a treat we must deny ourselves. Beaumont, toying with his recollections, writes to Jonson :—

" Methinks the little wit I had is lost
Since I saw you ; for wit is like a rest
Held up at tennis, which men do the best
With the best gamesters : what things have we seen
Done at the Mermaid ! Heard words that have been
So nimble, and so full of subtle flame,
As if that every one from whence they came
Had meant to put his whole wit in a jest,
And had resolved to live a fool the rest
Of his dull life."

Refreshed by a cup of canary, we press on to St. Paul's, just having time to glance along Paternoster Row, blocked by the coaches of ladies at the doors of its mercers' shops, passing the Pulpit Cross, newly enclosed with brick, and catching sight of the goodly inn of the Bishop of London. Our eyes wander to the booksellers' shops, though gaily-dressed men are hurrying past us. In the window of the Green Dragon is a black-letter copy of *Pericles.* At the sign of the Fox we may buy the *Merry Wives of Windsor;* at the Angel, the *Midsummer Night's Dream.* Apprentices pause to look at them hungrily, and rotund country gentlemen, up for law term, wonder inwardly what can interest us in these rubbishy plays. A passing Puritan righteously shrugs his shoulders, and leaves us to perdition. He is waiting impatiently for the preaching at the Cross.

Glorious St. Paul's is near us. It is a brave building, covering three acres and a half, and shining like a dream of clear stone amongst the dark fantastic houses surrounding it. We enter to see "the humours" of the time, and, as we have no spurs, the choristers at the door do not trouble us for a fine. Its double row of Gothic arches, the immense vista, the motley crowds taking their walk, impress us strangely. Was ever sight like this in any church in Christendom? Hundreds of people are parading up and down in their grand costumes, rattling their velvet-cased and gold-tipped rapiers, tossing their feathered hats, throwing back their laced cloaks to show their huge gold chains, shaking their beards, toying with their love-locks, whispering, swearing, hiring servants ("I bought him in St. Paul's," says Falstaff, of Bardolph), talking of the new play and the last pamphlet, the exploits of Drake, the whims of Philip of Spain. They are Paul's men, or Paul's walkers, the fashionable loungers of the day and their imitators, the wits and gulls, the roysterers and the thieves; needy men seeking a patron, the lover reading his sonnet to a friend, the incomparable dandy fluttering the town with his last foreign doublet or his copatain hat. Truly, as Dekker has it, "whilst devotion kneels at her prayers, doth profanation walk under her nose in contempt of religion." Characters disperse and re-arrange themselves like the bits of glass in a kaleidoscope. Puritans, with texts of Scripture embroidered on their shirts; the nobleman acquiring an appetite for his ordinary at the tavern hard by; the country squire, wondering and strange; the thief and the scholar; the learned doctor and the rustic; the priest and the player, in black serge and red silk; the sea-captain in blue; the Italian count in cherry velvet; the dusky slave in his cotton turban; and the Spanish grandee ablaze with jewels and gold, all mingle together for the student of life and character, who may find here his Hamlet and his Mercutio, his Tybalt and his Romeo. What a rich world it is to study—a world of comedy, romance, even tragedy. A similar scene may be witnessed in Temple Church, and even in Westminster Abbey.

But even those who greatly dare must dine, and so we betake ourselves to Tarleton's ordinary, in Paternoster Row, to discuss venison, fowl, and custard, watching the Paul's men smoking between the courses, and drinking huge beakers of ale or sack. After dinner, there are more "humours" to be seen. We stroll down Fleet Street, watching the jovial loafers entering the Devil's Tavern, looking for houses famous as the homes of living men, at the Fleet Prison, at the exhibition of sea-monsters, at Autolycus peddling his wares, at the gay coaches passing to the Strand, at the merry, brightly-dressed, jostling, ever-shifting crowd. Courtiers are returning from Whitehall; the vizored men on horseback have been to the tilting in St. James's Park; the man with the gay striped dress is a falconer, who has been flying his peregrines and Barbary birds at St. Mary-le-Bonne; the two scarlet-gowned, solemn-looking gentlemen, in the coach yonder, are the Members for the City of London, who have been discussing politics at Westminster; the feather-hatted gallant, whose horse plunges down Chancery Lane, is Wriothesley, Earl of Southampton, a friend of Shakespeare, to whom he dedicated "Venus and Adonis," going to his house in Holborn; opposite to us, but on the other side of Temple Bar, is Essex House, where Spenser says, "I gayned gifts and goodly grace," and he and Shakespeare were frequent visitors; and yonder are burghers' pretty wives, more lively than discreet, who come to look at the fine ladies and gentlemen, winning frowns from the former, and pretty hand-kissing from the latter. The eye is fatigued with the moving colours, the strange scenes and pageants. Life is a holiday to half the people we see about us; some are hurrying to the play, others to the bear-baiting, and all are merry, or tinged with that musing which is itself a luxury. We turn into the Temple Gardens, our player-friends having long since wended their way homeward for the afternoon performance at the Globe. After seeing the evening parade in the Exchange, and supping at the Pope's Head, we, too, must make our way back to Bankside.

As we muse on London Bridge at midnight—the chimes of St. Clement's have just finished—we can say with Falstaff, "We have heard the chimes at midnight, Master Shallow." Let us gather up some of our impressions of the City. The streets are narrow, ill-paved, with no causeways, and street-posts to protect the passengers from horses and vehicles. The narrower they are, the more silent below, the more full of whispering gossipers above, talking scandal from the windows of the upper storeys. In rain or sun we can walk beneath the storeys and signs unharmed. From the upper windows lanterns are hung at night, when the watchmen cry, on great occasions, or as trouble is brewing, "Hang out your lights!" But the shadows are deep, and many a crime is committed in them whilst Dogberry is idling after a cut-purse, thinking it the wisest plan "to let him show himself what he is and steal out of his company."

Whistling at night is forbidden, and the Statutes of the Streets are intended to keep strict order, and, of course, fail. Brawls and roystering are common. The steam of good things has saluted our nostrils as we have passed the taverns, where fat ale-wives have been briskly taking testers and changing crowns. Listen! Our musing is broken by the sound of a tenor voice. It is a lover serenading his mistress from the steps of her mansion by the water. He sings:—

"Who is Sylvia? What is she,
  That all the swains commend her?
Holy, fair, and wise is she;
  The heaven such grace did lend her
That she might admiréd be."

The moon peeps out, and there is a Juliet, leaning out of her balcony, to look on the beautiful Thames, and dream of her Romeo. Lights twinkle on the river—it is a party of gallants, returning from the Bear-garden, chatting, laughing, and smoking their silver-headed pipes.

Once more we return to our collections. Surely we have been at a masked ball of Shakesperean characters. They troop before us: Dr. Caius, Mercutio, Benedick, Autolycus, Moth, Falstaff, Pistol, Malvolio, Shallow, Shylock, Sir Armado, Costard, Trinculo, Mrs. Page, Rosalind, Portia—we seem to have had glimpses of them all. We have seen some of the gay mansions that lift their castellated fronts to the sky, and have left their names upon our streets and thoroughfares. The pages of the great book wherein Shakespeare read have been turned over for us, with their pageantry and pathos, their vice and ambition, their many-sided illustrations of life and character. Scraps of conversation, familiar words, references to current topics, specimens of foreign beaux and ladies, have made it easier for us to understand how the quick wit which studied in London should seem to have visited so many countries and filled so many professions. Here he passed the brightest years of his life, picturing what he saw, as well as bodying forth "the forms of things unknown."

When we come to dwell upon it, the references to London in the historical plays are of a most striking character. They show that the poet was familiar with its noble mansions as well as its taverns and streets. He places scenes in the Tower, at Whitehall, at Westminster Sanctuary, at York Place, in the Temple Gardens, at Baynard's Castle, at Ely House, at Crosby Place, at Gloucester House, and several other inns of note. The player associated with noblemen as well as roysterers of taverns and the wits of his own circle. He lived a rich, full, and varied existence. As for the dramatist, he was always busy, studying mankind, reading books, penning sonnets, composing plays, and probing his way into men's hearts and the mysteries of invisible things.

CHAPTER X.

THE DRAMA.

Miracle and Guild Plays—Interludes and Masks—Royal Players—Companies of Children—The Pageants—Court Revels—Strolling Players—Inn Yard Theatres—Noblemen's Companies—The First London Theatres—A Peep at the Globe During Play-Time—Poverty of Dress and Scenery—Parts Played by Shakespeare—Purpose of the Stage.

THE people had been trained in musical, mimetic, and spectacular representations. The early miracle-plays, or mysteries, were at first performed by ecclesiastics, in their churches, as they continued to be up to and even after the Reformation. Queen Mary revived them to teach the faith in which she believed, but under Elizabeth they were more rarely presented, and were tinged with Protestantism. There can be little doubt that they did their work effectually. Unable to read, the common people required some visible and vocal instruction. But the impulse which developed into the drama came from the Trade Guilds, in whose hands the miracle-plays passed into a new phase, and prepared the way for the semi-humorous allegories, out of which the comedy was gradually evolved.

The guild-pageants were regularly exhibited in the streets of London (where the parish clerks took part), Coventry, York, Chester, and other old cities. York had fifty-seven such pageants, and Chester, twenty-four. Each guild had its movable scaffold, on four wheels, consisting of a lower room, curtained from the public, in which the performers apparelled themselves, and an upper room, open to the sky, in which the piece was played. The scaffold was wheeled to some broad part of a street, or an open place (Toft Green, in York, was anciently known as Pageant Green), where stages were erected for the more important spectators. The performances were carefully gone through, in the presence of the city officials and the holiday-keeping citizens. On great public festivals several pageants would be proceeding at the same time, in different streets, white-capped women and children looked on from the overhanging storeys of their dwellings. Quaint-costumed men stood in the street, and passed their comments on bakers, tanners, carpenters, and cooks, who were personating patriarchs, angels, devils, or abstractions, to the best of their ability. The pasteboard properties, the scenes and accessories, were of the simplest description. Long after the guilds had ceased to be of much use for trading purposes, they continued to give annual performances. But most of them ceased to exist in the early part of Shakespeare's life.

Other causes were working in the same direction. The wealthy nobles still lived with their large establishments about them, taking their meals in the common hall, bound to their dependants by softened feudal ties, and entertaining their friends and visitors in magnificent style. It was no uncommon thing for a nobleman to dine several hundred persons, and to give them good amusement afterwards. Interludes, masks, and revels, were common on these occasions. The first were designed to show the conflict between good and evil, and introduced impersonations of Vice, Justice, Wisdom, and other abstractions. A strong humorous element ran through them, and the domestic clown had a prominent part assigned him. So elastic was the term interlude, however, that it covered any kind of non-religious representation. Pyramus and Thisbe, rehearsed by Snug, Bottom, and his friends, in *A Midsummer Night's Dream*, is described as an interlude of ten words. It is represented as being played at the wedding of Theseus, Duke of Athens, and Shakespeare is careful to distinguish Quince as a carpenter, Snug as a joiner, Bottom as a weaver, Flute as a bellows-mender, Snout as a tinker, and Starveling as a tailor, in obvious ridicule of the old guild-players. Philostrate, the master of the revels, describes them as "hard-handed men" who had "never laboured in their minds till now," when they have done so to honour the Duke's nuptials.

The humour of the cast and the rehearsal is inimitable. The instructions about the wall afford us a whimsical sample of the old properties. The lovers talked through a chink in the wall. But "you can never bring in a wall," says Snug. Bottom replies that "some man or other must present wall; and let him have some plaster, or some loam, or some rough-cast about him to signify wall, and let him hold his fingers thus, and through that cranny shall

Pyramus and Thisbe whisper." A man with a lantern represents Moonshine, and the comments on his appearance may be taken as illustrating the by-play, and perhaps the most amusing part, of these interludes :—

Moonshine. "This lantern doth the hornéd moon present."

Theseus. He is no crescent, and his horns are invisible within the circumference.

Moonshine. "This lantern doth the hornéd moon present; Myself the man i' the moon do seem to be."

Theseus. This is the greatest error of all the rest. The man should be put into the lantern; how is it else the man i' the moon?

Demetrius. He dares not come there for the candle; for, you see, it is already in snuff.

Hippolyta. I am aweary of this moon: would he would change!

Theseus. It appears, by his small light of discretion, that he is in the wane; but yet, in courtesy, in all reason, we must stay the time.

Lysander. Proceed, moon.

Moonshine. All that I have to say is, to tell you, that the lantern is the moon; I, the man in the moon; this thorn-bush, my thorn-bush; and this dog, my dog.

Demetrius. Why, all these should be in the lantern; for all these are in the moon. But, silence; here comes Thisbe.

When Falstaff, in response to Prince Henry, at the Boar's Head in Eastcheap, stands for his father, taking the chair for his state, a dagger for his sceptre, and a cushion for his crown, and delivers himself of a short speech, the hostess exclaims, "He doth it as like one of these harlotry (or common) players as ever I see." An interlude was, in fact, almost anything from a morality play to the antics of a tumbler, or the random wit-shooting of a clown. The more elaborate performances, however, resembled plays; but they were reserved for important occasions.

THE ACTING OF ONE OF SHAKESPEARE'S PLAYS IN THE TIME OF QUEEN ELIZABETH.

Heywood's interludes were short farces, and they introduced the characters of living men and women.

Masks and revels were also common, more especially at court and during the royal progresses. There was a Master of the Revels, with a fee of ten pounds a year, in Elizabeth's time. It was his province to have the royal plays, interludes, and masks, rehearsed before him, to provide the dresses and properties, to hear the children in their parts, and to prepare a written explanation for the Sovereign of all the devices employed, such as Philostrate handed to Theseus. The musicians, players, and costumiers, looked to him for their fees. The Queen's establishment consisted of eighteen trumpeters, six violinists, six flute-players, six sackbut-players, ten singers, four interlude-players, with three keepers of bears and mastiffs, costing altogether £1,289 12s. 8½d. per annum. The interlude-players, who were distinct from the Queen's players proper, received £3 6s. 8d, a-year in wages, and £1 2s. 6d. for liveries. This may not seem magnificent remuneration, but, if Flute is to be believed, "sixpence a-day during his life" would have "made" Bottom, as one of Duke Theseus's interluders. The mask was a diversified production, combining declamation and dialogue, with music, songs, dancing, and scenic effects. The masks of Jonson, Dekker, and Ford, are now almost forgotten, although clever and sometimes brilliant; but the *Comus* of Milton remains to remind us of its best and purest style. The mask was to modern opera what the interlude was to modern comedy.

Whether at Windsor or Richmond, or on her visits to her wealthy nobles, Queen Elizabeth was constantly entertained by acted shows, or by other diversions. Her secretary, Walsingham, writing to Mr. Herbert, in 1575, says, "Nothing is thought of at court but banqueting and pastime." Besides the establishment already mentioned, the Queen had four companies of children who performed for her amusement—the children of St. Paul's, the children of Westminster, the children of the Chapel, and the children of Windsor. The Children of the Revels were a public company, who performed at Blackfriars Theatre. Shakespeare alludes to these children-players in *Hamlet.* Rosencrantz says, in the conversation preceding the entry of the players, in reply to Hamlet's inquiry whether the actors have suffered as the result of the late inhibition, evidently referring to the plague, "Nay, their endeavour keeps in the wonted pace; but there is, sir, an aery of children, little eyases, that cry out on the top of the question, and are most tyrannically clapped for 't; these are now the fashion, and so berattle the common stages (so they call them) that many wearing rapiers are afraid of goose-quills, and dare scarce come thither." At first the child-players only acted the semi-classical pieces; but when they became public performers they were ambitious enough to set ordinary dramas.

The performance of the pageant proper required large numbers and some skill. Captain Cox and his Coventry troupe represented the massacre of the Danes before Elizabeth at Kenilworth, in 1575. English and Danish knights, mounted on war-horses, engaged in fierce spear-thrusts, mimicking a real battle, and even finishing by single combats on foot with short swords. Foot-soldiers followed the horse with striking and complicated evolutions, and, finally, the Danes were beaten, and English women appeared leading some of them captive. The players were rewarded with two bucks and five marks. In nearly all these performances the author, or arranger, was called into the royal presence and rewarded.

The later masks were extremely fantastic. Lakes and islands, woods and towers, hills and towns, clouds and stars, were artificially constructed to aid the illusion. Inigo Jones was extremely clever in the production of these artifices. The royal books are full of amusing entries that may reveal, by selection, something of the nature of the devices employed:—"A castle for ladies and a harboure for lords;" "dishes for devil's eyes;" "devices for hell and hell-mouth;" "a jebbett to hang up Diligence;" "a cotte, a hatt, and buskins all over covered with fethers of cullers (coloured feathers) for Vanytie, in Sebastian's play;" "the scythe of Saturn;" and "a periwig of heare for King Xerces' sister," are especially noticeable. At a midsummer show, in York, in 1584, the Corporation records give account of charges for "prickinge of the songes" sung by the Minster choir, and for "armes paintinge about the hearse in the first pageante, a crowne for the angell, spangells for his shirte, the mendinge of the Queenes crowne, one of the furyes bare, with some other trifells." At one of the masks of Elizabeth there was to have been a combat in the air, in the midst of which "legs and arms of men, well and lively wrought, were to be let fall in numbers on the ground, as bloody as may be;" but heavy rain prevented the display.

Sometimes the machinery did not work satisfactorily. Sir Dudley Carlton, writing of the Christmas festivities in 1604-5 says, "There was a great engine at the lower end of the room, which had motion, and in it were images of sea-horses, with other terrible fishes, which were ridden by the Moors. The indecorum was that there was all fishes and no water." A still more extraordinary scene is depicted by Harrington, at the mask given by King James, in 1606, when Christian IV., King of Denmark, visited England. The representations were intended to depict the arrival of the Queen of Sheba at the court of Solomon.

"The lady who did play the Queen's part did carry most precious gifts to both their Majesties; but forgetting the steps arising to the canopy, overset her casket into his Danish Majesty's lap, and fell at his feet, though I rather think it was in his face. Much was the hurry and confusion; cloths and napkins were at hand to make all clear. His Majesty then got up and would dance with the Queen of Sheba; but he fell down and humbled himself before her, and was carried to an inner chamber, and laid on a bed of state, which was not a little defiled by the presents which the Queen had bestowed on his garments; such as wine, cream, jelly beverage, cakes, spices, and other good matters. The entertainment and show went forward, and most of the presenters went backward, or fell down; wine did so occupy their upper chambers. Now did appear, in rich dress, Hope, Faith, and Charity: Hope did essay to speak, but wine rendered her endeavours so feeble that she withdrew, and hoped the King would excuse her brevity: Faith was then alone, for I am certain she was not joined with good works, and left the court in a staggering condition: Charity came to the King's feet and seemed to cover the multitude of sins her sisters had committed. . . I ne'er did see such lack of good order, discretion, and sobriety as I have now done."

Shakespeare's *Othello* was written in the early days of the reign of James, and he makes Cassio, after the "sport and revels" commanded by Othello, in consequence of "the mere perdition of the Turkish fleet," not only an example of the drunken reveller, but a protestant against the customs connected with such affairs. Cassio says to Iago, "O God! that men should put an enemy into their mouths to steal away their brains! that we should with joy, pleasance, revel, and applause, transform ourselves into beasts." Devices, processions, music, and mechanical ingenuities, made the masks so expensive that one of them, written by Chapman, and mounted by Inigo Jones, entailed the sum of £1,086 8s. 11d.

The indebtedness of Shakespeare to the revel-books for some of his plots is pretty evident. But we can be much more decisive as to the figurative allusions. For example, Antonio says:—

"Sometimes we see a cloud that's dragonish,
A vapour sometimes like a bear or lion;
A towered citadel, a pendent rock,
A forked mountain, or blue promontory,
With trees upon 't that nod unto the world,
And mock our eyes with air; Thou hast seen these signs,
They are Black Vesper's Pageants."

The familiar passage in *The Tempest*, written a few years later, is still more striking. Prospero observes to Ferdinand and Miranda, after Iris, Ceres, and Juno, have appeared, and the dance of the nymphs is over :—

> "You look, my son, in a moved sort,
> As if you were dismayed; be cheerful, Sir,
> Our revels now are ended. These our actors,
> As I foretold you, were all spirits,
> And are melted into air, into thin air:
> And like the baseless fabric of this vision
> The cloud-capped towers, the gorgeous palaces,
> The solemn temples, the great globe itself,
> Yea, all which it inherit shall dissolve,
> And like this insubstantial pageant faded,
> Leave not a rack behind. We are such stuff
> As dreams are made on, and our little life
> Is rounded with a sleep."

It has been fairly inferred that Shakespeare was present at the Kenilworth revels in 1575, when Elizabeth was so grandly entertained there, and he was in his twelfth year. All Stratford would be sure to go. Lakes and seas were represented in the mask. Triton, in the likeness of a mermaid, came towards the Queen, says George Gascoyne, and "Arion appeared sitting on a Dolphin's back." Arion's song, remarks Laneham, was a "ditty in metre so aptly endited to the matter, and after by voice deliciously delivered" that "with what pleasure (Master Martin), with what sharpness of conceit, with what lively delight this might pierce into the hearers' hearts, I pray ye imagine yourself as ye may." With these hints before us, and our knowledge of "young" Leicester's love for the Queen, there is no difficulty in seeing in the dialogue between Oberon and Puck, in

A Midsummer Night's Dream, distinct recollections of Kenilworth.

> *Oberon.* My gentle Puck, come hither: Thou remember'st
> Since once I sat upon a promontory,
> And heard a mermaid on a dolphin's back,
> Uttering such dulcet and harmonious breath,
> That the rude sea grew civil at her song;
> And certain stars shot madly from their spheres,
> To hear the sea-maid's music.
> *Puck.* I remember.
> *Oberon.* That very time I saw (but thou could'st not)
> Flying between the cold moon and the earth,
> Cupid all armed; a certain aim he took
> At a fair vestal, throned by the west;
> And loosed his love-shaft smartly from the bow,
> As it should pierce a hundred thousand hearts:
> But I might see young Cupid's fiery shaft,
> Quenched in the chaste beams of the watery moon;
> And the imperial votaress passed on
> In maiden meditation, fancy free.

It was impossible these scenic and allegorical displays should fail to stimulate the popular taste for regular characterisation. Little by little the men and women, the topics, the events, the fashions of the day, were introduced in interludes and diversions. Workmen, fascinated by their temporary successes, left their trades to engage in the romantic life of the strolling player. The Bottoms and Snugs, the Snouts and Starvelings, the Flutes and Quinces, wandered from place to place, attending weddings, fairs, festivals, and revels, to perform such pieces as they had learned. The player-booth of our childhood is one of the survivals of this vagabond-life. The players usually wore their costumes as they journeyed, and many a rough rustic wit must have made merry over a tawdry king driving a tilted waggon, or a queen squatting on the furniture, or cooking a dinner by a roadside fire, or a spangled angel, munching brown bread in large mouthfuls, or Cupid riding a mule, or the clown, who so frequently represented Vice, walking composedly by the side of the horned and hoofed Devil, whom it was his duty to torment on the village green for the moral edification of the unlettered. According to common report, Ben Jonson played the part of Hieronimo, in Kyd's tragedy of that name, with a company of strolling players, and, clad in his leather doublet, drove the waggon containing the stage properties. Even tradition, malicious as it sometimes can be, has inflicted no such indignity on the memory of our national bard.

As yet there were no theatres. In the towns, dramatic representations were given in the council chambers and guildhalls, if by regular noblemen's players, or in the yards of inns, most of which were quadrangular, and convenient for that purpose. In London there were such performances at the Cross Keys, in Gracious (now Gracechurch) Street, at the Boar's Head, Aldgate, at the Horse's Head in Cheapside, at the Bull in Bishopsgate Street, and at the Belle Sauvage, Ludgate Hill, prior to 1570. It was the same in the provinces, for Blomfield tells us, in his "History of Norwich," that the White Swan Inn, "over against the steeple, is an ancient inn, and the playhouse for the Norwich company is in this yard." The early theatres were modelled on the inn-yards.

The court-yards, in which the common people, or the groundlings, stood, became the pit, and the small galleries round the yard, where the better spectators were accommodated, were the precursors of boxes and galleries. A temporary stage was erected in the inn-yard when the gallery at the end was inconvenient. Many country inns still retain these galleries round the yard.

One of Elizabeth's first enactments was intended to restrain the abuses connected with these wandering companies. Performances were to be licensed by mayors, magistrates, and lords lieutenant, and no plays were to be performed "wherein either matters of religion, or of the governaunce of the estate of the common weale, shall be handled or treated"—a clear proof that the comedy proper was growing out of the interludes. Besides the unknown and inferior players, no doubt guild-actors in the first instance, there were sets of actors passing from one corporate town to another, belonging to noblemen, who took them under their patronage and protection. Eventually, it was enacted that the strolling-players, "not belonging to any baron of this realm, or towards any other personage of high degree," were to provide themselves with licenses from two justices, or be deemed rogues and vagabonds. Letters of authorisation, under the hand and seal of their master, were carried about by the noblemen's players.

The Queen's players, as distinct from her interluders, were appointed in 1583. The other chief companies in existence belonged to the Earls of Leicester,

Warwick, Nottingham, Sussex, Essex, Derby, Hertford, Pembroke, and Worcester, Lords Strange, Howard, and Clinton, the Lord Chamberlain, the Lord Admiral, and Sir Robert Law. Several of these companies played at Stratford-on-Avon in Shakespeare's youth. The Queen's players and the Earl of Worcester's were there in 1569. The Earl of Leicester's were present in 1573, the Earl of Warwick's and of Worcester's in 1574, the Earl of Leicester's and of Worcester's in 1577, Lord Strange's and the Earl of Essex's players in 1579, and the company of the Earl of Derby in 1580. In 1587 the Queen's players, otherwise known as Burbage's company, visited Stratford-on-Avon, and as it was with this company that Shakespeare was afterwards connected, it is fair to assume that the visit influenced his decision to go to London, and try his fortune as an actor and a poet. This explanation, at any rate, is far more consistent with his after-career, as a sensible man who could save money, than any more romantic legends and traditions.

The dispute between the Earl of Leicester's players, who had the Queen's patent to play anywhere, and the Corporation of the City of London, led, in 1576, to the construction of the first regular theatre, at Blackfriars, where James Burbage, the father of Richard, the tragedian, made a convenient house out of several rooms. The City officials were much annoyed. They complained that it had not previously been thought meet that players "should make their living on the art of playing," that public

THE FORTUNE THEATRE, GOLDEN LANE, BARBICAN.
(From J. T. Smith's "Antiquities of London.")

morals would be affected, and that large assemblages would spread the plague. Some ingenious and not creditable efforts were made to connect the plague and the players. Alliteration is always seductive, but it rarely suggests doctrine, as it did in the present instance. An unknown preacher packed the whole matter into a syllogism. "The cause of plagues is sinne, if you look to it well, and the cause of sinnes are playes; therefore, the cause of plagues are players." He might have made a better play on the sin of neglecting sewers, the folly of permitting filth, and the dire diseases developed from Fleet Ditch.

The temporary interdiction of performances during the plague did not prevent the building of other theatres. Ten theatres were in existence at the close of the century. The public theatres were the Globe, in Southwark, 1594; the Curtain, Shoreditch, 1576; the Red Bull, in St. John's Street; and the Fortune, in Shoreditch, 1599. The private theatres were Blackfriars, 1576; the Cockpit, in Drury Lane; and the Whitefriars, 1576, on Bankside. The Swan, the Rose, and the Hope, were smaller places. The Globe was hexagonal in shape, open to the sky in the centre, and thatched over the boxes. The private theatres were generally roofed in, lit by candles, and had evening performances. At the public theatres the representations were at one or two in the afternoon. Only one piece was played, lasting about two hours. The prices were—the pit, 6d.; and its front, or best, places, as high as 2s. 6d.; the boxes, 1s.; the galleries, 2d. Plays were acted on Sundays as well as other days, until 1583. At least two hundred persons styling themselves players were then living in London. "Yt is a wofull sight," wrote an intelligencer, or collector of news, to Secretary Walsingham, in 1586, "to see two hundred proude players jett (strut or walk jauntily) in their silkes, wheare five hundred poore people starve in the streets." The Queen's players wore scarlet cloaks, with velvet capes, in public. Shakespeare's plays were only performed at the Globe and Blackfriars.

Let us take a peep into the Globe. On one of the posts dividing the carriage from the footway is a play-bill. Apprentices, foreign-looking merchants with well-bronzed faces, a dandy staining his lace ruffles with snuff from a silver box, and a broad-shouldered countryman, evidently up for law-term, are conning its rough large letters. If we look over the shoulders of one of the apprentices we can read it. There is now being performed, it states, "The most excellent historie of *The Merchant of Venice*, with the extreame crueltie of Shylocke, the Jewe, towards the sayd merchant, in cutting a just pound of his flesh, and obtaining of Portia by the choyse of three caskets, as it hath diverse times been acted by the Lord Chamberlain, his servants. Written by William Shakespeare." There is no cast of the performers. "Ah, Shakespeare's a merry fellow," sighs one of the youths, who has evidently been struggling between duty and inclination, and finds the former too strong. He departs, and others of the group go to the door, pay their money, and enter.

We enter after them, in good time for the play. This is the wooden O, mentioned by the bard himself in his Prologue to *Henry V.* The pit is already fairly filled, and worth studying. Leathern-belted apprentices abound—some with permission of their masters, others, to judge from their dissipated looks, evidently without. Some are grouped in busy gossip on the earthen floor, others are playing at cards, whilst eating, smoking, chaffing, and hustling, are going on all round. There is a good deal of pushing towards the front. These are the "youths that thunder at the playhouses, and fight for bitten apples," referred to in *Henry VIII.* A few women, wearing masks, are visible here, but they rise no higher than the wives of citizens, and some of them sink much lower. In the boxes, whose fronts are hung with painted cloths, are the more fashionable persons, curled and perfumed, looking down on the tumult below with great curiosity. In a high box is the band, playing an overture, in response to a trumpet call, but not much regarded. The instruments apparently are shawms, violins, sackbutts, and dulcimers. The worsted stage curtain is down, and we can see that it opens down the centre, and that each part draws back from behind. Whilst the groundlings are pointing out the notables in the boxes—a well-known courtier, a new ambassador, a great sea-captain--the trumpet sounds again, and the curtain is drawn aside.

We are introduced to a street in Venice, as appears by a label in antique type. Had there been a prologue, it would have been spoken by an actor in a long black cloak, and had it been *Hamlet* or *King Lear*, the stage would have been hung with black. The stage itself is rather broad than deep. It is covered with green rushes. A curtain at the back hides a raised balcony, in which are unemployed actors, and possibly Shakespeare himself. The actors speaking wear common clothes, suitable to their rank in England. Before Bassanio enters, several dandies, in trunk hose and short cloaks, and dainty low-crowned hats, have lounged on to the stage, with boy attendants bringing their stools. Their rosetted shoes are plainly visible as they cross their legs, with an air of languor, and lift their eyebrows the better to study the pit. One of them, dreadfully bored, discards his stool, and lies all his length on the rushes. Another takes out his pipe and his tobacco, and begins to smoke through his nose, and to blow the blue cloud upwards, in ring after ring, to show that he has learned to "take tobacco" from the very best professors.

The play proceeds. Portia and Nerissa are played by boys, as are all women's parts. Presently Shylock enters in his Jewish gaberdine, such as can be seen any day in the Jewerie, or in Lombard Street, and there is fierce clapping in the pit. Surely, it is Richard Burbage himself. The dandies on their stools seem momentarily interested. One takes from his pocket his table-book, made of small pieces of slate, bound together in duodecimo, such as Autolycus sold in *A Winter's Tale*, and such as Sir Nathaniel drew out to write down the most "singular and choice epithet" used by Holofernes, in *Love's Labour's Lost*, in describing Don Adriano de Armado as being "too picked, too spruce, too affected, too odd, as it were, to peregrinate." We are unable to see what he is writing down, whether comments on the play, or passages for use in conversation at St. Paul's, or over his ordinary. Probably his friends will hear him saying to-night, "How like a fawning publican he looks," "The devil can cite Scripture for his purpose," or "In religion what damnèd error, but some sober brow will bless it, and approve it with a text." Concerning the dandies turned critics, Ben Jonson once wrote: "Let them know the author defies them and their writing-tables." Many of the pithy quotations still in common use were first introduced by the writing-table gentry, who made them classic before the plays in which they were contained were printed for public reading.

Amidst whistling from the select sitters on the stools, and much yelling from the pit at Shylock, and a good deal of merry imitation when Bassanio sings, in the casket-scene, the play goes on. The sprawling gentleman, who is evidently ill at ease, wishes the audience to see that he cares nothing for Portia and her domestic arrangements, and so he crosses the stage at the back, and joining another exquisite on the opposite side, they fall to cards, to pause for a few minutes whilst a jester appears, between the third and fourth acts, to dance a jig, and sing a rude snatch full of what are now called "topical allusions." The trial scene comes on, and down go the cards into the rushes. The pit is still as the grave. All eyes are on the stage. A bystander whispers in our ear, "The Duke is played by the author, a right noble-looking fellow." We recognise him at once. He delivers himself with effect, in a soft but round mellow voice. One or two table-writers are busy with their slates the scratching of their pencils distinctly audible in the pauses of the dialogue. The performance at length comes to an end. The players come forward to the front of the stage. They kneel together, and say, in concert, "God save the Queen," as the Epilogue says himself, in the Second Part of *Henry IV.*, and as it used to run at the end of our own playbills. The curtains cross together, and amidst hooting, jostling, and chaff, the crowd disperses. Presently Shakespeare and his companions will go to the Falcon, or cross London Bridge for a night at the Mermaid, pointed at as they pass, and individually as well known as rotund Jonson and reverend-looking Chapman.

Such, with small variations, was the play-acting of the days of Elizabeth and James. There was abundant time after it was over for the idlers who cared to spend more hours in amusement. The Bear Gardens, the Cockpit, and the Pawn, were always accessible. Movable scenes were sometimes employed, but not very frequently. "Piece out our imperfections with your thoughts," suggests the Chorus in opening *Henry V.*:—

> "Think when we talk of horses that you see them
> Printing their proud hoofs i' the receiving earth."

Confessions of this inadequate representation occur in other places. The wonder is that for such small audiences, and under such conditions, a man of Shakespeare's genius cared to write and act dramas at all. The promise of immortality for work done under similar conditions would hardly be regarded as sufficient recompense by an ambitious modern playwright. But, no doubt, the plays were well acted, and well patronised, and the enthusiasm of the audience would be both a stimulus and a reward.

More imposing scenic effects on the stage followed the successes of Inigo Jones with mechanical masks. It was at one of these displays, in 1613, when the Globe Company was acting *Henry VIII.*, that the firing of small cannon lit the thatch of the roof, and burnt down the theatre. The dresses on this occasion were described by Sir Henry Wotton as being of such splendour "as to make greatness very familiar if not ridiculous." But they were not usually remarkable except for meanness. Their poverty is referred to by more than one writer of the day. The court dresses were lent to noblemen for their festivities, and when the University of Cambridge, in 1594-5, wanted to play a tragedy for "the exercise" of the scholars, they requested the loan of "ancient princely attire, which is nowhere to be found but within the office of the Robes of the Tower." No wonder, then, that poor players represented Brutus and Cassius in the Spanish cloak of the period, and dressed for kings and princes like the dandies about town. Players earned from 17s. to as much as £6 a week. The profits were usually divided at the Globe and Blackfriars, where £20 was a large receipt for a full house.

Elizabeth never visited any of the public theatres. Very few respectable women ever did, or there would have been less coarseness in the plays of the time, which may be said to have been written solely for men. But she frequently had Shakespeare's pieces played before her. She was a great admirer of the two parts of *Henry IV*. *Othello* was played before her in 1602. Eight of Shakespeare's plays were performed before King James, in 1603—4, at Hampton Court, and in the banqueting-house at Whitehall. *Macbeth* was performed before him several years after, and contained a complimentary reference to him in Macbeth's lines :—

> "I'll see no more :—
> And yet the eighth appears, who bears a glass
> Which shows me many more ; and some I see,
> That two-fold balls and treble sceptres carry."

No authentic information can be obtained respecting the letter King James is said to have written to the poet, and it must have perished. But it was probably suggested by Macbeth.

Shakespeare himself played the Ghost in *Hamlet*, Adam in *As You Like It*, and the English kings he so masterly portrayed. Referring to the last, John Davies, a contemporary, says :—

> "Some say, good Will, which I in sport do sing,
> Hadst thou not played some kingly part in sport
> Thou hadst been a companion for a king,
> And been a king among the meaner sort."

There are references in his sonnets to certain repugnances connected with his profession which may have a moral value. In the one hundred and tenth he says :—

> "Alas ! 'tis true, I have gone here and there
> And made myself a motley to the view,
> Gored mine own thoughts, made cheap what was most dear,
> Made old offences of affections new."

In the next sonnet he says :—

> "Oh ! for my sake do you with Fortune chide,
> The guilty goddess of my harmful deeds,
> That did not better for my life provide
> Than public means, which public manners breeds ;
> Thence comes it that my name receives a brand,
> And almost thence my nature is subdued
> To what it works in, like the dyer's hand."

Shakespeare was no wild libertine, flashing out a play between one debauch and another, like Marlowe, or living amidst the stings of conscience or the wiles of pleasure, like Green. Chettle speaks of his demeanour as being "no less civil than he excellent in the quality he professes ; besides, divers of worship have reported his uprightness of dealing which argues his honesty, and his facetious grace in writing that approves his art." This was written in 1593, whilst the poet was still in London, in reply to Green's malicious reference to him as a "Johannes Factotum," "a shake-scene," "an upstart crow beautified with our feathers," a "tiger's heart wrapped in a player's hide." His purpose, in play-writing, was to do something more than amuse. His stories are full of reality, pathos, and direct teaching. His works have been called "a lay Bible." In his own words, "The purpose of playing, whose end, both at the first and now is, to hold, as 'twere, the mirror up to nature ; to show Virtue her own features, Scorn her own image, and the very age and body of the time, his form and pressure."

CHAPTER XI.

LITERATURE OF THE PERIOD.

Its Excellence a Revelation to Europe—Euphuism the Counterpart of Fantastic Dress—Shakespeare's Miscellaneous Reading—His Indebtedness to Others—The Solid Works of the Time—Pamphlets—Miscellaneous Poetry—Spenser—Dramatic Literature nearest Popular Heart—Early Dramas—Shakespeare's Contemporaries—His Sudden Rise to Eminence—Contemporary Allusions—Complete View not Possible in his Lifetime—The England of his Birth and Death.

THE literature of Elizabeth's reign was as much a revelation to Europe as the exploits of Drake on the Spanish main, or the mighty chase of Castilian vessels from the Lizard to the northern seas. Its variety, splendour, and originality, were a surprise. With all their love of good eating and fine clothes, Englishmen had displayed a refined taste for classic learning, a quick sense of the picturesque in language, and a range of creative genius, that commanded the admiration of Western Europe. The halls of courts and castles were not only converted into academies, but the printing-press gave forth productions in prose and verse, criticism and chronicle, romance and tragedy. Italian novels and romances were sold at every shop in St. Paul's Churchyard, and even found their way to the provincial capitals. Purists, like Roger Ascham and John Lyly, might lament that these foreign enchantments were "marring men's manners," but, without them, literature would have lost its stimulus and conversation its charm.

The "euphuism" of conversation, as it was called, from John Lyly's book, had been borrowed from the Italian Republics. It was the intellectual complement of the external taste. Dress was gaudy in colour and fantastic in style, and conversation was florid, tricksome, and affected. Men and women never wearied of displaying their learning in alliteration, citations, quips, and puns. They experienced a proud delight in

> "Talking of stones, stars, planets, of fishes, flies,
> Playing with words, and idle similies."

The opposite of euphuism, the introduction of ancient and uncouth words, is justified by the poet Spenser in his preface to the "Shepherd's Calendar":—"As in the most exquisite pictures they used to blaze and portrait not only the dainty lineaments of beauty, but also round about to shadow the rude thickets and craggy cliffs," he says, "even so do these rough and harsh terms enlumine, and make more clearly to appear the brightness of brave and glorious words." The two streams of influence are plainly discernible in nearly all Shakespeare's writings. They were natural. His country speech gave strength and fibre to the cultivated "ornation," as Grindal styles it, of more intellectual conversation, as the freshness of his metaphors came, like the breezes from the hills, to the weary town-folk who listened to his plays.

Shakespeare was "poor in dead school-cram," as

Augustus Schlegel pithily expresses it; but he possessed "a rich treasury of living and intuitive knowledge." He was evidently familiar with the best literature of his time. Webster, in his dedication to the *White Devil*, in 1612, refers to "the right happy and copious industry of Master Shakespeare," intending to mean more than the amount of his work; and there is no doubt that he read intelligently and constantly. The growth of power, insight, and concentration, in his dramas, is proof of it. The Italian romances, the English chronicles, the rhymed histories, the old ballads, the current poetry, and the dramatic works of his day, may all be traced in the composition and allusions of his plays. Milton's idea of him, warbling "his native wood-notes wild," is passable; but Hume's account of him as "without any instruction either from the world or from books," is only excelled in its absurdity by Voltaire's description of his *Hamlet* as "the work of a drunken savage."

Scarcely an eminent Greek or Latin author had been left untranslated for the benefit of English readers. From Plutarch Shakespeare obtained the materials of his *Timon of Athens;* his *Macbeth* suggests Æschylus; and his *Comedy of Errors* is founded on the story of the *Menæchmi* of Plautus. From Bandello, an Italian novelist, he borrowed the idea of *Much Ado About Nothing;* Cinthio, another Italian fabler, supplied him with hints for *Measure for Measure* and *Othello;* *Cymbeline* was partly obtained from Boccaccio, with an admixture of British legend; and there are traits, touches, and incidents, in his other plays that could not have been produced without the aid of other current romances. Beatrice, in *Much Ado About Nothing*, says Benedict declared that she had her good wit out of "the Hundred Merry Tales," compiled from Italian authors, and published in England in 1557. Geoffrey Fenton's "Tragical Discourses" were drawn from similar authors, and an accompanying commendatory poem set forth—

"Now men of meanest skill, what Bandel wrought may view,
And tell the tale in Englishe well that erst they never knewe;
Discourse of sundrye strange and tragicall affaires,
Of lovinge ladyes' helpless haps, theyr deathes and deadly cares."

Sir John Harrington had also enriched our literature with a rendering of the "Orlando Furioso" of Ariosto, with its "new stores of fiction and imagination, both of the romantic and comic species, of Gothic machinery and familiar manners." From the depth of his retirement in the forest of Knaresborough, Edward Fairfax had sent to the world his unrivalled translation of Tasso's "Jerusalem Delivered." Of foreign materials there was thus a rich abundance for poet and play-writer.

More solid works were not wanting. Froissart's "Chronicles" had been published in 1523. Fabyan's "Chronicles" were read by private tutors to their pupils. Holinshed's "English Chronicles" had made their appearance in 1577. Daniel's "History of England," to the time of Edward III., and Sir Walter Raleigh's "History of the World," were popular works. Hakluyt's wonderful book of voyages had been completed in 1598. An account of the voyage and shipwreck of Somers, and others, on the Bermudas, was published a little before the writing of the *Tempest*, which it evidently suggested or shaped. Knolles's "History of the Turks" was also published, from which Shakespeare drew many of his impressions; and whence, still later, according to the poet's own admission, came "the Oriental colouring" of Byron's mind and poems.

Sidney's "Apology for Poetry" and Puttenham's "Art of Poetry" were pleasant and profitable dissertations. Character-sketches, showing how the drama was affecting ordinary literature, were published by Hall and Overbury. Philip Stubbes's "Anatomy of Abuses," a rather exaggerated attack in dialogue on the prevailing styles of dress, manners, and amusements, had made some stir in 1583. Harrison, Stowe, Camden, and Speed, had described the character, the incidents, and the physical aspects and general life, of the country. At least ten of Bacon's essays were printed during Elizabeth's reign, though the complete number did not appear until later, and his "Novum Organum" was not presented to King James until 1620. Foxe's "Martyrs" had appeared in 1563; Jewel's "Apology of the Church of England" in 1562; four books of the judicious Hooker's "Ecclesiastical Polity" in 1594, and the remainder in 1618. Witty John Donne, one of the members of the Mermaid Club, published his "Pseudo Martyr" in 1610.

As yet there were no newspapers. If statesmen wanted to collect news, or to feel the national pulse, they employed intelligencers, who mixed with the crowd at St. Paul's, and listened to the familiar talks at the ordinaries. It was the early age of the pamphlet. If a Puritan wished to gird at a Papist, if a profligate, like Green, cared to "lay open his loose life," if a politician had ideas and suggestions that burned for expression, he wrote a pamphlet. Poor John Stubbes, who expressed in this way the popular antipathy to the marriage-scheme between Queen Elizabeth and the Duke of Alençon, had his right hand chopped off with a cleaver, on a scaffold before Westminster Palace, in the year 1579; his printer, Page, being punished in the same fashion. The newspapers supposed to have appeared in 1558 are seen, by their water-marks, to be forgeries.

Poetic literature was varied and copious. The "Mirror for Magistrates," a rhymed selection of tragical stories, by various writers, begun in Mary's time, had been printed in 1559 and 1563. It was considered a work every accomplished man should read. Another poetic miscellany was "The Paradise of Dainty Devices," consisting of one hundred and twenty-four poems, written by several persons. Edwardes was the chief contributor, and the stanzas Peter quotes in *Romeo and Juliet,* about music, with its "silver sound," are from one of his poems. In 1576, George Gascoigne, described in a petition against him, in one of the Domestic State Papers, evidently by a bitter enemy, as "a common rhymer, a notorious ruffian, an atheist, and a godless person," produced his "Steel Glasse," a long and minute satire on the time, written in blank verse, the first important poem of an undramatic character which appeared in that dress. Sir Walter Raleigh's first verse was written in praise of this poem. He said—

> "This Glass of steel impartially doth show
> Abuses all to such as in it look,
> From prince to poor, from high estate to low.
> As for the verse, who list like trade to try,
> I fear me much, shall hardly rise so high."

Raleigh's other verses were sweet and fluent. Nor can we omit a reference to Sir Philip Sidney's "Reformed Poetry," or English verse in Latin measures. Cowper has borne fine testimony to the latter's "Arcadia," a compound of prose and verse, when he speaks of Sidney —"warbler of poetic prose." Quaint Fuller, replying to the critics of the same work, happily retorts, "Such who say that his book is the occasion that many precious hours are otherwise spent no better, must acknowledge it also the cause that many idle hours are otherwise spent no worse, than in reading thereof." Dyer, the author of "My Mind to me a Kingdom is," Greville, and Daniel, a personal friend of Shakespeare, who imitated his sonnets, were minor poets of the time. Michael Drayton, a Warwickshire man, is now more known for his "Polyolbion," a poetical description of Britain, than for his minor pieces, though they possess considerable sweetness. The Elizabethan age was indeed "a nest of singing birds," and the smaller poems were full of quaint pathos, religious fervour, and even national spirit. "Much of the verse written, and more or less valued in Elizabeth's reign, has passed away," observes Professor Morley. "The very good remains, but of the good perhaps there has been as much lost as preserved."

The first poet of the time, outside the drama, was unquestionably Edmund Spenser. He was a Londoner by birth and education, but his great poem, "The Faëry Queen," was written in Ireland. The nine comedies he wrote on the Italian models, and which his friend, Gabriel Harvey, thought came "nearer Ariosto's comedies," are completely lost, whilst the allegory slighted by the latter is immortally associated with the name of his friend and the literature of England. The poem itself is a delicious medley of Platonism, Puritanism, and classic mythology, written in a stanza named after its author. It harmonised with the adventurous spirit of the time, it was full of allegorical presentations of its people and its tendencies, and it reflected the central idea of the great national struggle, the triumph of the true over the false religion, though it was the Puritanism of Archbishop Grindal and not the Protestantism of Elizabeth that he idealised. The poem appeared during Shakespeare's residence in London. He mentions its author by name in his "Passionate Pilgrim," as the representative of "sweet poetry."

> "Spenser, to me whose deep conceit is such
> As passing all conceit, needs no defence.
> Thou lov'st to hear the sweet melodious sound
> That Phœbus' lute, the queen of music, makes,
> And I in deep delight am chiefly drowned
> Whenas himself to singing he betakes."

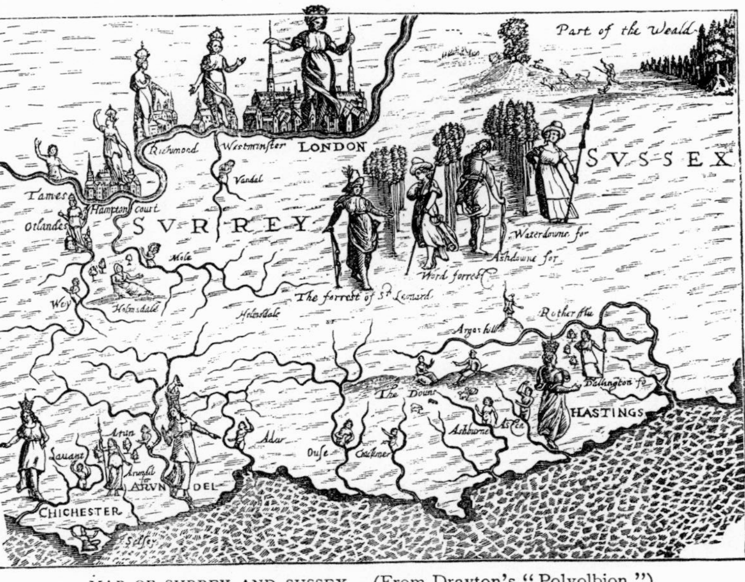

MAP OF SURREY AND SUSSEX. (From Drayton's "Polyolbion.")

A new poet, a thoroughly English singer, a Christian symboliser, had made his appearance in Spenser. That Shakespeare discerned his worth must be accounted to his credit by even the dainty æsthetics who can find little to commend in his own plays. The culture and fine sensibility, shot through and through with fibres of almost martial vigour, that characterise "The Faëry Queen," ought to make it much more frequently read than we fear it is at the present day. The closing line of its dedication to Queen Elizabeth, "To live with the eternitie of her fame," is a prophecy whose realisation we all admit. His other poems must be passed over here. In the Tyrone rebellion of 1598, his home at Kilcolman was sacked and burnt, because of its former associations. Flying from the foe, he reached London, to die there, in King Street, Westminster, of starvation and a broken heart. It is pleasant to think he would have had relief from Bankside had his real condition been known, and that Shakespeare himself may have shed a tear over his remains when they were consigned to Westminster Abbey.

The dramatic literature of the time was nearest to the popular heart and life. It reflected the virility of speech and manners. It bore witness to the emancipation of the nation from its religious restraints and its European narrowness. It was permeated with the new nationalism that saw its birth in the past and its hopes in the future. It was full of the quick-breathing intellectual eagerness, the abounding humour, and the literary frolic, which seem so astonishing in their richness to classic formalists, or the critics of a colder age. Of the earlier dramatists, there was a Nicholas Udell, the head-master of Eton, who flogged Latin into his boys with a cane, and then wrote a comedy for them to replace Plautus and Terence. This was *Ralph Roister Doister*, a rough, whimsical production, introducing popular characters, and not without considerable merit. It was based on the Latin models, but was vastly inferior to many comedies produced in London a few years later. *Gorboduc*, the first real English tragedy, was the joint production of Thomas Norton and Thomas Sackville, for the Christmas festivities of Lincoln's Inn, in the year 1561. It was founded on the events which Geoffrey of Monmouth narrates subsequent to the story of King Lear. It was played before Queen Elizabeth, at Whitehall, in January, 1562. Thomas Preston, another University man, was the author of a drama called *King Cambyses*, to which Falstaff refers, in the First Part of *Henry IV.*, when he says to the Prince, "Give me a cup of sack, to make mine eyes look red, that it might be thought I have wept; for I must speak in passion, and I will do it in *King Cambyses*' vein."

But these and similar productions were all eclipsed by the plays which were the talk of the town when Shakespeare reached London. Marlowe's *Tamburlaine the Great*, from which Pistol quotes incorrectly, as from memory, the passage about "pampered jades of Asia," in the Boar's Head scene of the Second Part of *Henry IV.*, and his *Doctor Faustus*, powerful, but turgid, and storm-and-pressure dramas, had made

Kit famous. The Barabas of his *Jew of Malta* was hereafter to be purified of its grossness and its ferocity in the Shylock of Shakespeare, as his *Edward II.* was the forerunner of the historical plays in which Shakespeare was to prove that he might have been a pupil, but that he had no real master. Some of the plays of Robert Green, a writer as riotous and profligate as Marlowe, were also current. But, perhaps, he owes the preservation of his name more to the fact that he was the author of the only unkind reference to Shakespeare himself that has been penned than to anything original in his poems, his nouvelettes, or his plays. The "upstart crow," who thought himself able "to bombast out a blank verse," had only written two or three plays when Green died, jealous of his fame. Kyd's *Hieronimo* and Whetstone's *Promos and Cassandra,* which seems to have suggested *Measure for Measure,* had been represented at the theatres before the arrival of "gentle Willy." Amongst the other miscellaneous pieces for the stage prior to 1588 were Lyly's comedies of *Alexander and Campaspe,* and *Sappho and Phaon;* Peel's *Arraignment of Paris;* Lupton's *All for Money;* Wilmot's *Tancred and Gismund;* Gascoigne's *Supposes,* from which Shakespeare borrowed the name of Petruchio; and John Still's *Gammer Gurton's Needle.*

The Elizabethan drama, as we know it, was not yet formed. But it was visibly growing into shape and volume. As soon as the idea of writing English comedies and dramas had become common property, the rate of production seems to have been considerable.

Probably the plays current and produced in the Shakespearian period would number several hundreds. A group of active dramatists were formed during Shakespeare's residence in London, consisting of famous men. There was mighty Marlowe, robust and wild; there was George Chapman, "the proud full sail of whose great verse" Shakespeare praises in his sonnets; there was rare Ben Jonson, the heavy-built, good fellow, whose fame is only second to his master's; there was Dekker, who had written thirty-two plays, none of which are read nowadays, except by the curious. There was Middleton, who suggested in his *Witch* the supernatural machinery of *Macbeth;* there was poetic Massinger, of whose thirty-eight plays only eighteen have escaped destruction; there was Webster, an extravagant, terror-rioting Shakespearean; and there were those twin-brothers in song, Beaumont and Fletcher. Fifty lesser men were writing plays, but they have written in vain, for few persons know their names or care to read their works. The play was not usually published until some time after its production on the stage. A drama, sold to the public players, fetched twenty nobles, or £6 13s. 4d. Private companies paid more. It was to the interest of the holders of the manuscript to prevent publication, or to sell it themselves to the booksellers. The customary fee for a dedication was forty shillings. Like all the other works of the time, the plays were printed in black letter.

Into the midst of this throng of needy and active spirits Shakespeare pushed himself bravely, at once a student of life and plays, of acting and of actors, an author, a manager, and a man of mark. He won personal respect for his "uprightness of dealing." He did not plunge into the daring licentiousness of Green and Marlowe, much as poetic anatomists may dissect confessions of misdeeds from his sonnets. He read, thought, and composed, with industry, vividness, and fluency. His best work was done in London, and within ten years of his arrival here he had made a name, established his supremacy in the drama, and produced some of his immortal works. Writing in his "Wits' Treasury," in 1598, this is what Francis Meres says of him, in words that will bear quotation, familiar as they are to many readers:—

"As the soul of Euphorbus was thought to live in Pythagoras, so the sweet, witty soul of Ovid lived in the mellifluous and honey-tongued Shakespeare; witness his 'Venus and Adonis,' his 'Lucrece,' his sugared sonnets amongst his private friends, &c. As Plautus and Seneca are accounted the best for comedy and tragedy amongst the Latins, so Shakespeare among the English is the most excellent in both kinds for the stage; for comedy witness his *Gentlemen of Verona*, his *Errors*, his *Love's Labour Lost*, his *Love's Labour Won*, his *Midsummer Night's Dream*, and his *Merchant of Venice*; for tragedy his *Richard II.*, *Richard III.*, *Henry IV.*, *King John*, *Titus Andronicus*, and his *Romeo and Juliet*. As Epius Stolo said that the Muses would speak with Plautus's tongue if they would speak Latin, so I say that the Muses would speak with Shakespeare's fine-filed phrase, if they would speak English."

We may also gather from other contemporary allusions in what estimation he was held. John Weever, in 1595, styled him "honie-tongued Shakespeare," and in 1601 wrote that "the many-headed multitude were drawn by Brutus' speech," and John

Marston, in 1598, compliments him on "his well-penn'd playes." An anonymous author of the *Return from Parnassus*, in 1601–2, complained that the university-penned plays were too classical, adding, "our fellow Shakespeare puts them all down, I and Ben Jonson too." In his "Baron's War," Michael Drayton saw in him "all sovereign powers," and declared :—

> "When heaven his model first began,
> In him it showed perfection in a man."

In 1603 Chettle sang of him as "silver-tong'd Melicert," and "the sweet singer Corydon." The poet Spenser praised him as "pleasant Willy," in his "Tears of the Muses":

> "— he, the man whom Nature's self hath made
> To mock herself, and Truth to imitate."

But the crown of all was Ben Jonson's poem, "To the Memory of my Beloved Master, William Shakespeare." The dead bard is invoked as "the soul of the age," "alive still while thy book doth live," "not of an age, but for all time," his mind and manners shining "in his well-tunéd and true-filéd lines."

But no complete view of his mind and influence was possible in his lifetime. Some of his best plays remained buried in prompters' books. No newspaper existed to announce the advent of a new poet. In the provinces, it is doubtful whether his name would be known at all as that of a man of note. To the general world he was simply one of a race of play-writers, who had more skill and judgment than his fellows.

That he would live when they were dead and forgotten would have seemed at best a doubtful proposition. That eminent men would come from all parts of the world to see his birthplace would have been scouted as impossible and ridiculous. He was certainly clever, graceful, subtle, and penetrating. Sententious passages from his works were in common use, as the salt of conversation. Later writers compared themselves with his famous characters. The ancient families treasured his early volumes, and the gravy stains and "thin flakes of pie-crust between the leaves" proved, as Steevens says, that "most of his readers were so chary of their time, that (like Pistol, who gnaws his leek and swears all the while) they fed and studied at the same instant."

The full measure of his orbed greatness, however, had yet to dawn upon England and the world. Only eighteen of his thirty-six or thirty-seven authenticated plays were published in his lifetime. His immediate personal friends, with the exception of Jonson, were not fully conscious of his transcendent merits. In issuing the first folio edition of his entire plays, in 1623, seven years after his death, his two friends and fellow-actors, John Heminge and Henrie Condell, referred to them as "these trifles," and dedicated them to the Earls of Pembroke and Montgomery, who had been pleased to think well of them. They expressed regret that the author himself had not lived "to have set forth and overseen his own writings," and they describe some of the previous editions, the quartos, as "stolen and surreptitious copies, maimed and deformed by the frauds and stealths of injurious impostors." They professed to offer to the public the real works, "cured and perfect of their limbs, and all the rest absolute in numbers, as he conceived them." He is himself described as "a happy imitator of nature," and "a most gentle expresser of it." It is added that "his mind and hand went together; and what he thought, he uttered with that easiness that we have scarce received from him a blot in his papers." The second folio edition appeared in 1632, and it was followed by two others. But it was not until the next century that editors and critics, of known fame and capacity, made their appearance, and that Shakespeare began to be regarded as our greatest national bard. His learned contemporaries had not recognised in him any such faculty, if they had ever thought of him at all. Bacon never mentions him, nor yet Hobbes, who outlived him by half a century. It had not been "suspected," either by his friends or his successors, that he was, as Emerson finely expresses it, "the poet of the human race; and the secret was kept as faithfully from poets and intellectual men as from courtiers and frivolous people." Yet he was himself the inspirer of much of our subsequent literature, and a very sun, thawing the frost-bound energies of German intellect, fully a hundred years after the grave had closed over him at Stratford-on-Avon. As Emerson adds—"Now, literature, philosophy, and thought are Shakespearised. His mind is the horizon beyond which at present we do not see."

The England of our day is what it is because

Shakespeare had being in the age of Elizabeth, as well as because we have had wise sovereigns, shrewd patriots, astute men of science, and fervid moral and religious reformers. His influence upon us has been constant and vast, the glory of a sun, the weight of an atmosphere, the force of gravitation. It had begun to mould and pervade men's thoughts and feelings in his own day. The England of his birth had been a paltry power, shut out from the East and West Indies, unable to claim the dominion of the sea, plotted against by the Pope, divided by hostile factions, impoverished by social changes, destitute of adequate expression in letters and song, and wanting the pulse which follows successful endeavour, the genius which is born of half-realised aspiration. The England of his death had been baptised with a new spirit. It had been trained to finer issues under the guidance of a woman of heroic mould. The glory of Spain had been crushed, the empire of the sea had been won. The Vikings it had reared had founded Colonies, and left their names on far-off lands and Continents. Europe had been astonished with its vitality and fibre. It had blossomed into riper self-consciousness; it had become a nation sovereigns would have to learn to respect. Shakespeare had taught it history in his chronicle plays, and it was a fortunate thing that the events of the past had not yet been treated, as Schlegel remarks, "in a diplomatic and pragmatic spirit." He was thus able to sound a note that still rings, in phrase and quotation, in moments of patriotic enthusiasm or counsel. He had educated the unlettered in public affairs, and revealed to them, in flashes, the life of other lands. They could understand Cæsar, Antony, and Timon, if it required a more advanced people to realise Macbeth and appreciate Hamlet. In the Shakespearean drama, in fact, England had found a new world for its ranging, rich with the spoils of conquest, studded with happy isles, laved by sunny seas, and flecked by fantastic sails.

INDEX.

Acted Shows before Elizabeth, 180
Agricultural produce, where sold, 40
Alum in Yorkshire, 47
"Anatomy of Abuses," by Stubbes, 88
Apothecary of Shakespeare, 119
Apple trees in Devonshire, 29
Armada, Composition of, 100
——, Preparations for reception of, 100
——, its terrible doom, 101
Armour, dress and weapons, 95
Army and navy, 14
—— of England in 1588, 98
Articles revised and reduced, 104
Ascham's testimony to Elizabeth's discernment, 148
Astrologers at country fairs, 124
Astrology, Belief in, 123

Bacon and his "Advancement of Learning," 118
—— on Englishmen, 15
Banks for relief of necessity, 49
Bankside and Globe Theatre, 160
Beaumont and Fletcher, 214
Beech, Use and price of, 26
Beer and wine, Consumption of, 84
Ben Jonson a strolling player, 186
—— on Shakespeare, 216
Beverages or "nuntions," 80
Boorde, Dr. Andrew, 120
—— his medicines and prescriptions, 120
Bowls an unlawful game, 91
Bowyers and Fletchers, Origin of, 91
Bread Street and its inns, 165
Bridges in England, 22
Building in England, 20
Bull-baiting and cock-fighting, 88
Burleigh and Cambridge students, 75
"Butlerage" on foreign wines, 51

Calais, Loss of, and Consequences, 41
Cards and dancing, 86
Carlton on Christmas masks, 182
Cassio, example of drunken reveller, 183
Castles, their condition, &c., 32
Cathedral Establishment, 105
Cavendish, Thomas, Career of, 58, 59
Cecil on the cloth-makers, 43
Chancery Lane and Wriothesley, 168
Charges at theatres, 192
Cheapside, Description of, 164
Chelsea and Pimlico hamlets, 155
Children, Treatment of, 114
—— of the revels, 180
Church ales, 88
—— preferments, Sale of, 149
Cures suggested by superstition, 121
Cities of England, 19
City of London : its taverns, 161
Classic compliments, 148
Clink, Liberty of the, 161
Closing of churches, 103
Cloth trade of England, 42
Coaches, Introduction of, 85
Coal trade in England, 46
Coinage in England, 39
Combativeness of common people, 80
Common spirit of Englishmen, 98
——, Training rendered easy by, 98
Companies of London, 40
Company of Tripoli Merchants, 40
—— of New Trades, 40
—— of Eastland Merchants, 41
Compliments of the time, 147
—— paid to Shakespeare, 215
Comus, a mask, 179
Cooks from France and Italy, 82
—— called "atheists" by Jonson, 82
——, their confectionery, 82
"Corn-badgers," 47
Corporation of Norwich, 1583, 20
Costumes of the time, 71
Court favourites, how rewarded, 49
Courtiers and counsellors of Elizabeth, 135
Courts of Elizabeth and James I., qualities of, 134
——, Marked difference between, 135
——, Characteristics and persons of, 135
Culverin and muschite, 96
Cutting of the hair, 75

Davis, John Doings of, 57
Dean Nowell at St. Paul's, 106
Dee, the Mortlake astrologer, 123
—— on reformation of calendar, 123
—— famous as an alchemist, 124
Domestic fools or jesters, 81

Drake, Sir Francis, Career of, 62
——, early services at sea, 62
——, his personal appearance, 63
——, first to sail round the world, 64
—— knighted by the queen, 65
——, expedition against Spain, 1585, 65
—— singes the King of Spain's beard, 66
—— captures the *Madre de Dios*, 66
Dramatic literature, 211
—— representations in Guildhall, 186
Drayton on decaying woods, 28
——, his description of the English counties, 30, 31
——, his "Polyolbion," 207
Dress of different ranks and classes, 73, 76
Duelling as if to music, 80
—— in the street, 79
Dutch opinion of Englishmen, 15
Dyeing and shape of beard, 75
—— in Coventry, 42

EARLY ENGLISH PLAYS AND PLAYWRIGHTS, 212
East Chepe and the Boar's Head, 162
Elizabethan drama, Rise of, 213
—— dramatic writers, 214
—— or Jacobean dandy, 74
Elizabethans unscientific, 117
Elizabeth, her accomplishments, 140
——, her adornments, 144
——, her attendants, 143
——, her appearance, 145
——, her body guard, 140
——, her costumes, 145
——, her dissimulation, 149
——, her extravagance, 71, 72
——, her inclination to Ritualism, 105
——, her popularity, 102
——, her parsimony, 148
——, her side-saddle, 144
England not a corn-growing country, 38
—— of Shakespeare's birth and death, 219
English history, 1564—1614, 17
Englishman's appetite famous, 81
Englishmen all the world over, 69
—— feared by Spaniards, 99
Essex House in the Strand, 168
Euphuism, its source, 201
Exchange at York, 45
—— or Bourse, 163

FACTS OF ELIZABETHAN AGE, 13
"Faëry Queen," Symbolism of, 110
Fans and high-heeled shoes, 72
Fairies and their dances, 128
Falstaff and Prince Henry, 176
—— on head-dresses, 73
Farthingales and stomachers, 72
Fee farm rent of Norwich, 82
Fences uncommon in England, 29
Fens of Lincolnshire, 31
Fern seed makes invisible, 132
Finsbury an archery ground, 152
Firearms, Kinds of, in use, 96
Fish-curing at Yarmouth, 45
Fishing trade, 53
Fleet Street and its loafers, 168
Flemings in Bermondsey, 44
—— in Isle of Axholme, 32
Foot soldiers, Equipment of, 95
Foreign fashions ridiculed by Shakespeare, 73
Forests in Elizabeth's time, 25, 26
Forks, Introduction of, 83
Frobisher, Martin, Account of, 57
——, his discoveries and services, 57
Froude's fable, 59

GARDENS OF OLD ENGLAND, 37, 38
Gascoigne's "Steel Glasse," 206
Gentleman piracy, 53
German opinion of Englishmen, 15
Ghost tales, Influence of, 131
Gilbert and terrestrial magnetism, 119
Gilbert, Sir Humphrey, Life of, 61
——, Pamphlet by, 61
——, his sad and sudden end, 62
Glass windows, 45, 86
Globe Theatre, Description of, 192
——, audience in pit, boxes, &c., 193
——, band, Composition of the, 193
——, stage and scenery, 194
——, spectators on the stage, 194
——, boys play women's parts, 194
——, conduct of the audience, 195
——, close of the performance, 196
——, dispersion of the audience, 196
"Good Queen Bess," 149
"Goodly Gautries," 26
Gorboduc, first English tragedy, 212
Grenville, Sir Richard, Exploits of, 69
——, his last fight and death, 69
Grindal and ordination, 106
Guild-pageants, 173

HARRINGTON'S ACCOUNT OF MASK GIVEN BY JAMES I., 182
Harquebus and petronel, 96
Harrison on English inns, 23
Harvey and circulation of blood, 119
Hawking and hunting, 88
Hawkins, Sir John, Career of, 59
——, originator of slave trade, 59
——, voyage of 1567 and result, 60
——, services against Armada, 60
Hawkinses of Devon, The, 58
Headless horsemen, 128
Heywood's interludes, 179
Hostelries on great thoroughfares, 23
Household arrangements luxurious, 85
Houses in provincial towns, 20
—— of the nobility, 35, 36

IGNORANCE OF LOWER CLASSES, 116
Immense potations, Cause of, 83
Indoor amusements, 86

Influence of immigration on English manufactures, 44
Interludes, Meaning of, 174
Internal defence, Regulations for, 92
Interior of country, 19
"Italionated," Meaning of, 108

JAMES I., HIS LOVE OF HUNTING, 139
——, his personal appearance, 149
——, his government, 149
Jewerie and Bucklersbury, 163
Joan of Arc, 127
"Johannes Factotum," 199

KENILWORTH REVELS, 1675, 184
Kersey-making in Leicester, 42

LACE-MAKERS AT CRANFIELD, 44
Lambeth and Faux Hall, 156
Land, 25, 39
Law, Study of the, 113
Learning at the universities, 112
Licences to collect alms, 48
Life in English mansions, 37, 80
—— of wealthy nobles, 174
Literature of Elizabeth's reign, 201
"Little Latin and less Greek," 114
Liverpool a poor port, 52
Lombard Street, 162
London Foreign trade, 40
London in comparison with Paris, Antwerp, and Venice, 151
—— an everlasting wonder to Englishmen, 152
——, External appearance of, 152
——, its walls and gates, 152
——, character of its exterior, 156
—— street boy, 163
——, references to, in Shakespeare, 171
London Bridge, its appearance, 161, 169
London stone in Cannon Street, 162
Longevity, Bacon's recipes for, 120
Lucky and unlucky days, 132

MAIDS OF HONOUR OF ELIZABETH, 143
Manners precise and fantastic, 79
Mansions of nobility, 20
Manufactures of England, 42
Marlowe's plays, 213
Marriage of the clergy, 105
Marriages of children, 79
Mary-le-Bonne Palace, 136
—— and Hyde Park, 155
Masked ball of Shakespearian characters, 171
Masks and revels, 174, 179
Mathematics despised by Bacon, 118
Meres on Shakespeare, 216
Mermaid, and club held there, 165
Military training and pastimes, 92
Mineral wealth of England, 46
Mines and iron mills, 28
Mining industries, 46
Miracle-plays or mysteries, 173
Monasteries and abbeys, 32
Monopolies and interference with trade, 48
Mounted troops, Equipment of, 96
Music, Influence of, on Elizabeth, 146
Musters of counties, &c., 95

NATURAL PHILOSOPHY, 118
Naval forces of England, 1588, 99
Nobility, middle classes, and commons, 14
Norwich, Manufactures of, 44
Nonsuch Palace, near Ewell, 139

OAK FORESTS IN ENGLAND, 27
Opposition to theatres, 187
Out-door pastimes, 87

PAGEANT PROPER AT KENILWORTH, 181
Pamphleteering, 205
Paradise of dainty devices, 206
Parish churches, Number of, 21
Paternoster Row, 166
Pauperism, Question of, pressing, 111
Pawn-banks—*Henry IV.*, pt. ii., 49, 50
Pavin or pavan, The, 87
Pears and vines in Gloucestershire, 30
Pelican and *Golden Horn*, 64
Performances at inns and hostels, 187
—— before King James, 198
Pews, Introduction of, 109
Physic and Queen Elizabeth, 120
Pies, pasties, &c., 82
Plants and animals, 132
Play-acting, *temp.* Elizabeth, 196
Players, 179, 198
Plots, &c., of Roman Catholics, 104
Pluck of English proverbial, 15
Polled sheep, a perilous beast, 128
Poor Law Acts of 1575 and 1601, 111
——, The new, 111
Portia on Falconbridge, 74
Poetic literature, 205
Portraits of Elizabeth, 145
—— of Shakespeare, Impressions produced by, 17
Postal communication, 24, 25
Poultry: why so called, 163
Preaching at St. Paul's Cross, 107
Precious stones, 122
Prices fixed by statute, 48
—— of provisions, 87
Printing-presses of Venice, 115
Privateering winked at, 53
"Prophesyings" and "Grindalisings," 106
Prospero, the magician, 129
Protestantism and piracy, 53
—— finally established, 102
Public schools, Condition of, 113
Puritan movement and "Faëry Queen," 109
Puritanism, Origin of, 110
Puritans, Wants of, 111

QUEEN'S COMPANIES OF CHILDREN, 180
—— players, The, 188

RALEIGH, SIR WALTER, STORY OF, 67
——, his various services, 67
——, why beheaded by James I., 68
——, his "History of the World," &c., 68
Rapiers, boots, and hats, 75
Richmond Palace, Surrey, 137
Roads, Condition of, 22, 23
Royal influences and English trade, 51
—— palaces, The, 136
—— parks, 36
—— progresses and their cost, 140
Ruffs, theme of Puritan satire, 76

SACK, OR SHERRIS-SACK, 84
St. James's Palace, 136
St. James's Park, 155
St. Paul's Cathedral, its appearance, and those who frequent it, 167, 205
——, Roof of, 26
Scotchmen in England, 25
Scott, Reginald, on witchcraft, 127
Sea dogs of Devon, 54
Seamen of Elizabeth's time, 54
Seaports of England, 19
Serenading by moonlight, 170
Sermons, Excessive length of, 107
Services in church, Variable, 107
Settlement, Law of, 111
Shakespeare and his age, 16
—— as an actor, 199
——, his belief, 108
——, his indebtedness to revel-books, 183
——, his industry, 202
——, his influence on his country, 219
——, sources of his plays, 203—207
Shakespeare's father, 15
"Shepherd's Calendar," Preface to, 202
Shooting with bow and arrow, 91
Sidney's "Apology for Poetry," 205
—— "Arcadia" and other poems, 207
Signs, omens, and presages, 130
Silver and base coins, 39
Singing in church, 108
Smelting at Dartford, 46
Society of Antiquaries, 122
Southwark and the Tabard, 156
Spenser, 208, 211
Spirits referred to by Shakespeare, 128
Spitalfields and Smithfield, 152
Starch, an invention of the devil, 72
Statutes of the streets, 170
"Sterling," Origin of term, 39
Strand and Temple Bar, 156
Strand-side houses, 159
Strength of Protestantism, 103
Street quarrels and duels, 79
Strolling players, 185
Sunday ill kept, 103
Supernaturalism, Effects of, 133
Superstition, Prevalence of, 129

TAILORS OF MARTIN-LE-GRAND, 74
Tarleton's ordinary, 168
Tea and coffee, Introduction of, 83
Temple Gardens, 169
Thames, Scene on the, 156
Theatres not visited by Elizabeth, 198
Theatres intended for men only, 198
——, their origin, 191
——, their condition, 191
Tilting and tournaments, 88
Timber in England, 27
Tobacco-smoking, 84
Tower, The, and Wapping, 152
Trade of the time, 51
Trading companies *temp.* Elizabeth, 40
Training to arms deficient, 95
Travel, 187
Travelling a feat, 22
Tumours, rickets, and king's-evil, 121

UDELL'S "RALPH ROISTER DOISTER," 212
"Unnecessary wares," 52
Uprightness of Shakespeare, 215
Use of cross-bow by ladies, 88

VEGETABLES LITTLE USED, 83
Villagers and manor-houses, 21

WALKER, ORIGIN OF NAME, 43
Washes and philtres, 121
Water, how conveyed, 20
Welcombe, Enclosure of, 29
Welshmen's hose, 73
Westminster a city by itself, 155
Wheat, Yield and price of, 39
Whitefriars and Alsatia, 159
Whitehall Palace, 156
Windsor Palace, 136
Witchcraft, Belief in, 125
Witchfinder, Occupation of, 126
Wool and corn of England, 38
Wool trade, staple of England, 39
"Working-house of thought," 112
Writers of Elizabethan times, 205, 207
—— of James's time, 206

YEW TREES, FOR WHAT USED, 27

THE END.

PRINTED BY CASSELL & COMPANY, LIMITED, LA BELLE SAUVAGE, LONDON, E.C.